Jihad of the Soul

Single Muslims Struggling With Identity, Religion And Desire

ZARINAH EL-AMIN NAEEM

The Niyah Company
KALAMAZOO, MICHIGAN
WWW.NIYAH.NET

Jihad of the Soul.

The Niyah Company

Printed in the United States of America

First Edition: November 2008

Contributors:

Questions for So You Wanna Know ™ - Cheryl El-Amin, LMSW

Copyright © A Letter to the Brothers by Halim Naeem, M.A.

Cover design by Tariq Abdullah of Tarchitects.org

Preliminary Editing by Idris El-Amin, Soheila Naeem, Tahira Naeem, Leslie Wade, Theresa Rutgers, Halim Naeem, Maurice El-Amin, Iman Khalid, and Cheryl El-Amin

ISBN 978-0-9822215-0-1

100% of the proceeds from the first 300 copies sold go to support the Girls Education in West Africa (Sierra Leone).

Visit our website at www.niyah.net

Send all Comments, Questions, and Suggestions to zarinahelamin@gmail.com

To Bami (Thelma Flowers) and Grandma (Amma Louise Ware),
two women who inspired me to be all that I am, can and will be.

And to Single Muslims around the world striving for the Siratul-Mustaqeem

ACKNOWLEDGMENTS

First, I acknowledge God for giving me the fortitude to complete this project. Secondly, I am indebted to my husband, Halim for his support, inspiration and insight, as well as putting up with my long hours....thank you! Thanks to Sufyan, our son who provided the smiles, hugs and laughter I needed to keep going.

From Western Michigan University, I deeply thank Dr. Ann Miles, my advisor whose wisdom and support was paramount to my success. To Dr. Chien-Ju Guh and Dr. Mustapha Mizeler, I thank you for reading draft versions and pushing me to explore important aspects I may not have otherwise investigated. I also owe an enormous dept to Dr. Kristina Wirtz, my committee member but also my fellowship supervisor. Thanks for helping me keep my workload and academic goals in perspective. Lastly, I thank Linda Comrie, Tony Dennis and the Graduate College for supporting my academic career through the Thurgood Marshall Fellowship.

To my support system, my friends and family (especially Mom, Dad, Maurice, Idris, Aunt Caroline, Umm Halim and Umm Murad) who either babysat Sufyan and/or gave feedback on aspects of my research, I love you all. To my parents who financially supported my work – thanks for believing in me! To Tariq of Tarchitechts, thanks for being so great to work with - I can't wait to have you design our house! And most importantly to my informants, thanks for your honesty, patience and support. I know for most of you this was your first time sharing intimate details of your life. I pray that Allah keeps us strong in our *iman* (faith) and dedication to good works.

Finally, this is a first edition and accordingly I want to thank in advance everyone who shall read and provide feedback on the project. In my quest to spark conversation, I look forward to hearing what you have to say. Thanks and Peace, ***Zarinah***.

PREFACE

Jihad an-Nafs (Jihad of the Soul)

> And as for him who fears to stand in the presence of his Lord and forbids the soul from low desires, then surely the garden -- that is the abode (Quran 79:40-41)

Jihad, an Arabic term, means to "strive" or "struggle." The Prophet Muhammad (peace and blessings be upon him) was quoted as saying the greatest *jihad* is the *jihad* of the soul - an individual's personal efforts to do right and to discipline themselves (in the sight of their Lord). It is the struggle to overcome temptations, carnal desires and evil, and to strive for the hereafter through worship and devotion. In this way, Muslim singlehood is a sort of spiritual and emotional battleground created from the intersection of various cultural wombs that present competing sets of values and expectations. The ambiguity, complexity and hybridity therein, generate manifold challenges and *"mini jihads"* for Muslim young adults of all backgrounds.

This book, *Jihad of the Soul*, presents these struggles and shows how being Muslim in a society that does not value your ideals can present a challenge. It also reveals the strategies of ideological resistance used by many Muslims to traverse this hurdle, and to defend against those aspects of life in America that conflict with their brand of a Muslim identity – e.g. popular sex culture. I aim to highlight the complexity of the lived experiences of American Muslims, and reveal the similarities, and differences between American Muslims and other Americans.

While research on Muslims is increasing, the general tone of many studies is in relation to terrorism and war. *Jihad of the Soul* reclaims the most important meaning of *Jihad* and addresses an issue that is of importance to Muslim young adults themselves: singlehood, something they worry about, dream about, and care about. This is their story, in their words.

CONTENTS

Jihad of the Soul

INTRODUCTION

Between Desire And Faith

This research on Muslim singlehood grew out of my own experiences as a young single Muslim struggling to balance religion, identities and desire. Though I am now married with children, well one child, there were times when my singlehood felt unbearable. I remember one flight home from Sierra Leone where I worked in international development. As usual in flight, I looked out over the clouds and began to feel as if my spirit was floating around me. I thought about the trip I had just made - my first tour as the Africa program coordinator for Life for Relief and Development, a Muslim non-profit organization. I thought about new friends, the resilient war survivors, the beautiful children and the gorgeous landscape. I thanked God for providing such an incredible experience. I truly felt blessed, but there was something missing. Where was my man? More specifically, where was my soul mate, my lover, the one to help fill in the blanks 20 years from now when during dinner conversation with friends I relive the experience? So while I loved the trip, I hated that I did it single. There looking out at the clouds, I prayed to marry soon so that the next time I was at 30,000 feet, my soul would have a companion.

God had another plan. Two years and three long trips passed before my prayer would be answered. Finding a spouse, a Muslim spouse who loved me and whom I loved, proved to be a bit difficult. I pondered just getting a boyfriend. I mean really, what was so different now? I could just get a boyfriend, hang out and ask him to accompany me on my next trip. At least my hand would be held during trying ordeals, or my mind would be comforted when I couldn't think of a great solution to a problem, or my body would be shielded during some dangerous situation, or, or… I complained, "*If I wasn't Muslim, I wouldn't be so lonely! I didn't have a problem getting a man until I decided to become a stronger Muslim.*"

May Allah forgive me! Really, from ninth grade to two years post-college I always had a steady man in my life. Those were the times when I dated (usually without guilt.) The times when neither religion, nor getting married were the first things on my mind.

Well times had changed. In college, I experienced a religious awakening and that old lifestyle no longer jived with my new "Muslim" soul, the "*Muslima*" (Muslim woman) Zarinah. This Zarinah was trying to live as a "good" Muslim–no more relationships without intentions of commitment.

So I waited. I waited to meet a Muslim husband like I met non-Muslim boyfriends before. I waited and I waited and I waited, until it became apparent that perhaps *no one* would approach me! *"What's the problem? Did my Islam suddenly bring on a case of the uglies? Is this a test from God? Am I being punished?"* Perhaps this wait was my scarlet letter, my living punishment for past sins. It may seem funny and far-fetched, but for someone who believes in the afterlife, it is not.

Literally, I cried on my Lord, "*Oh God, give me some respite! Who am I going to marry? Will he care that I haven't always been a "good Muslim?" You know I just started wearing my scarf right? Will he love children? Will he be outgoing? …. When are you going to answer me!?!?*"

From age 20 or so, I wondered if I would ever marry. I joked with my friends, *"Please pray for God to give me strength… I'm going crazy!"* Yes, I was active in the community, had a great job but was still so lonely. Then one day while overseas (alone again), my mother emailed about Halim, a single Muslim brother. Our beloved Sheik Ali (a local religious leader) was playing matchmaker and thought Halim and I may be compatible. I thought "*Why now while I'm overseas!*" But unbeknownst to me, my curious father met Halim and his father for lunch while I was away. Then when I returned home in April, Dad gave me the details: Halim was 22 years old (2 years younger than me I might add), from Ann Arbor, and was going to school for psychology. It took me a minute to get over the age difference, but we finally set up a family dinner for May. Halim came with his parents and we discussed everything from my strong personality to Halim's personal goals, to polygamy and the ways Halim planned to support his wife. I determined that "*Hey, he's Muslim, cute, intelligent, looks strong… why not give it a try?*"

We exchanged information and began to talk on the phone. It all worked out because by August, three short months later, we had set a marriage date for the following July. Yes, a fast process by most standards! Later when my grandmother's health deteriorated, we moved the wedding up so she could see her only granddaughter walk down the aisle. In November, just 7 months after our inaugural family dinner, we married and for the first time my soul had a legal mate. I could now enjoy all the comforts of male companionship without the accompanying unmarried religious guilt. I just might get into heaven yet!

Later, I suspect, because I openly discussed my struggles, Muslims of all ages began to tell me their singlehood experiences. They too were lonely and unable to find a spouse. Some struggled to "stay on the straight path" and maintain their Islamic identity, while others deemed "the Good Muslim path" too hard or simply unnecessary and chose to live a different lifestyle. Unlike me, some remarked that external, not internal pressure was the source of their discomfort (my parents never pressured me to get married). Overall, it was apparent that singlehood was a stressful period for many Muslims.

In response, my friend Marquia and I organized a singles event where Muslims could ask relationship questions and meet eligible singles. It was a success and even resulted in one marriage. Given these experiences, I later designed my research thesis around the topic that confronted my daily life: the singlehood of Muslim young adults.

DESIGNING THE STUDY

I originally conceptualized this study around a dichotomous relationship between ideal "Muslim" values and "American" values. I asked, "*How and why do Muslim young adults perform and maintain their religious identity in a society that does not hold the same values?*" However, I quickly discovered that to conceptualize the meaning of singlehood for Muslim young adults, I also needed to explore identity construction and salience- that is which identity is most prominent. Muslim identity versus American identity was too simplistic. There are several cultural fields (hereafter referred to as cultural wombs) and ideologies including Islam, society, personal experiences, spirituality, peers and parents which influence Muslim young adults (Beckworth and Morrow 2005). I would have to examine the intersection of religious identities with other identities affecting their singlehood.

So, I broadened my questions to address these issues identity salience and pluralism. The new research questions became:

1. How are Muslim identities formed, maintained and hybridized in a society of great religious and spiritual diversity?
2. What are the attitudes of Muslim young adults towards their singlehood and what are the factors that play a role in the formation of those views?
3. What are the challenges Muslim young adults face within their singlehood?
4. Lastly, how can the Muslim community address the issues raised?

To investigate these phenomena, I employed traditional ethnographic methods over a nine-month period (December 2007 – August 2008). I conducted interviews with 21 Muslim young adults aged 18-36, ranging from 30 minutes to four hours and several of whom I spoke with on numerous occasions. I was a participant observer within a variety of locales including local *masjids*, Muslim conferences and other Muslim events. I spoke with several parents, *imams* and other community members and analyzed American Muslim cultural documents such as magazines, websites and newsletters.

I discovered I was not alone! Irrespective of ethnic background, economic level, gender or geographic location, many single American Muslims had similar fears, concerns, feelings and needs. Sure, not everyone had problems. There were some who were very comfortable in their singlehood, but they were the minority. As a result, I adopted a critical lens and narrowed my findings to the most challenging aspects of Muslim singlehood.

Background on Singlehood in America vs Islam

Before we can delve right into Muslim lives, I must provide a bit of background. Traditionally, American marriage served to legitimize sex, authorize parenting, and provide an economic basis for two individuals (Stein 1975). As such, in 1957, 95% of the U.S. population over the age of 18 was married. Yet by 2006, according to the U.S. Census Bureau fact sheet, the percentage of married Americans aged 18 and over dropped to 59%. Why the shift? Stein, a pioneer of singlehood research, argues singlehood is not only a viable choice for many Americans, but that the emergence of singlehood as a lifestyle is most likely a response to a growing dissatisfaction with traditional marriage (1975, 1981). Exploring shifts in college students' attitudes about marriage, he found that 39% of college seniors felt traditional marriage was becoming obsolete, and 25% agreed that the traditional family structure of mother, father, and children living under one roof no longer works. At that time, the interest of Stein and others was to predict the probable decline of lifetime marriage.

> It is too early to predict with confidence that the increase in singleness among the young will lead to an eventual decline in lifetime marriage ... just as cohorts of young women who have postponed childbearing for an unusually long time seldom make up for the child deficit as they grow older, so also young people who are delaying marriage may never make up for the marriage deficit later on. They may try alternatives to marriage and they may like them (Glick 1975:18 in Stein 1975).

Indeed today, alternatives to marriage such as long-term cohabitation or habitual dating exist. It appears Stein was correct, for many, the ideological and economic bases for traditional marriage have been removed. "Men no longer (have) to marry to get sex and women no longer (have) to marry to get financial support" (Bird 1972 in Stein 1975: 491). The women's liberation movement that stressed achieving fulfillment outside of wife and motherhood, meant that it was socially acceptable for a woman to live a long comfortable life without a man. This, coupled with a high divorce rate, the advent of the birth control pill and other movements such as open marriages, gay liberation and communal living, broadened the common definition of American marriage. Relationships now often emphasize companionship rather than children and family and people are free to exert their independence (Stein 1975).

Stein's research is 20-30 years old but recent studies like DePaulo (2006) also suggest American marriage is quickly becoming obsolete. In "*Singled Out: How Singles Are Stereotyped, Stigmatized, and Ignored, and Still Live Happily Ever After,*" DePaulo, argues "while the institution of marriage is ensconced in the laws, politics, religions and cultural imaginations of Americans, it is presently of little true significance as a meaningful life transition" and is, in effect, inessential (DePaulo 2006:11). Financial stability and children traditionally achieved through marriage, are now socially available outside of marriage; a trend DePaulo argues removes the need for many Americas to marry.

Given the work of Stein and DePaulo, one may assume a majority of Americans have no desire to marry. However, it appears that is not the case. Several popular books and studies like Holland and Eisenhart (1990) suggest that marriage is still an important part of American culture. Nevertheless, whether desired or not, approximately 41% of Americans are single (U.S. Census 2006) and for many, singlehood is stressful and confusing.

In response to this phenomenon, popular books often attempt to show single Americans how to love, rather than lament, their singlehood. But there are gender differences. Women account for just over half (54%) of the single American population, (there are 86 men for every 100 women), yet single women are largely the targets of the "single and loving it" message. For example, Jerusha Stewart, one of America's 89 million singles, grew tired of feeling like the "last single girl in the world." After interviewing close to 200 singles, mostly women, about their choice to stay single, she discovered she was not alone. For several reasons, for many women the choice was less *when* to get married and more *if* to get married. She writes, "It's becoming more acceptable to consider education goals, career focus, and individual growth as important—if not more so —than love, marriage, and children" (Steward 2005:4).

> It's no accident that so many singles are happily avoiding the altar. While I would wager that only a small minority actually woke up one morning and declared, "I will never marry!", these mingling millions have consciously or unconsciously opted for another choice. Their everyday decisions, concerning where to work, what to wear and

> when to workout, have played a major part in how they live. For most women, it's been a gradual coupling of financial advancements and rising self-satisfaction with their single lives, which has resulted in their declaring their marital independence. Singles did not make a single choice. They seized a series of opportunities, which led them towards the sensational solo life (Stewart 2005: 4-5).

Stewart sees a single status as an asset and finds no reason to give up sensational singlehood for marriage. Her book includes quizzes and suggestions for everything from dating, starting a new hobby and blessing your home, to making a "morning-after sex" breakfast. Still, Stewart acknowledges that while singlehood can be fun, many women (including herself) truly desire marriage. She includes suggestions on how to find a man including being open and upfront in relationships and not afraid to share your true feelings and desires. Other books like, *Living Alone and Loving it* by Barbara Feldon (2002) and The Single Girl's Survival Guide by Imogen Lloyd Webber (2007) also aim to increase the well-being of single women.

Christian Singles

Numerous books address singlehood from a Christian perspective, often arguing for singlehood as God's gift and useful to increase God's work. However, like Islam, Christianity embraces and advocates for marriage, and these publications tread a thin line. According to Sinton,

> A key issue for Christian theology is what emphasis to give to singleness in relation to the state of marriage. Is it to be treated as pathological: something abnormal that requires either a cure or at least the alleviation of pain? Or should we emphasize it as a privilege: the special vocation of the truly devoted follower of Christ? The middle way is to view singleness and marriage as parallel states, each having their own particular joys and sorrows (VM Sinton in Farmer 1998:6).

One example is *The Rich Single Life*, by Andrew Farmer (1998) that uses biblical scriptures to argue against the stigma placed on singles (as shiftless or somehow less human). Like DePaulo, Farmer's argument begins with a discussion on ways singles are seen as deviant. He cites, "the good life is defined as marriage... any living arrangement is wrong that may make any marriageable individual forego marriage" (Mead 1967 in Stein 1975:489). He suggests this pervasive view of singlehood, makes many singles feel inadequate. Likewise, Barbara Holland, a single woman remarks, "Happily-ever-after has rejected us. The fairy tale story has spit us out as unworthy, and sometimes we suppose perhaps we are" (in Farmer 1998:6).

Muslim Singlehood is not only about sex. But a ban on premarital sex in a society where it pervades presents a challenge

Farmer wants single Christians to feel worthy and loved by God. He suggests that while married individuals' time is spent concerning "the affairs of this world" and pleasing their spouses, singles have more time to focus on pleasing their Lord. "Undivided devotion to the Lord," he argues, is the essence of a biblical identity for the single adult.

Interestingly, a similar view exists in Islam, in the story of a Muslim saint named Rabi'ah al-Adawiyya. Born around 717 C.E in what is now Iraq, it is said that Rabi'ah remained single to have what Farmer described as undivided devotion to her Lord. A poet, several of Rabi'ah's poems center on taking God as her lover:

My Beloved

My peace, O my brothers and sisters, is my solitude,
And my Beloved is with me always,
For His love I can find no substitute,
And His love is the test for me among mortal beings,
Whenever His Beauty I may contemplate,
He is my "mihrab", towards Him is my "qiblah"
If I die of love, before completing satisfaction,
Alas, for my anxiety in the world, alas for my distress,
O Healer (of souls) the heart feeds upon its desire,
The striving after union with Thee has healed my soul,

O my Joy and my Life abidingly,
You were the source of my life and from Thee also came my ecstasy.
I have separated myself from all created beings,
My hope is for union with Thee, for that is the goal of my desire.

American Muslims & Singlehood

So how do Muslims compare with the literature above? Stein (1981) identified four categories of never married individuals: 1) voluntary/temporary singles, 2) voluntary/stable singles, 3) involuntary/ temporary singles, and 4) involuntary/stable singles. Naturally, single Muslims fall into all four categories and move between and among them over their lifetime. However, Islam presents marriage as the ideal state for humankind. The Prophet Muhammad himself exalted marriage and advised his followers to marry - there are few stories of long-term celibate singles like Rabi'ah. Therefore, marriage is coveted and Muslim singlehood is deemed temporary. Of course, Muslims are not alone in this belief, other religious Americans like the Mormons, hold similar views (Darrington et al 2005).

Accordingly, my findings show that most college-aged Muslim young adults are voluntary/temporary singles. They plan to marry but are currently focused on school. Post-college however, most Muslim young adults become involuntary/temporary singles. They desire marriage and actively look for ways to end their singlehood. This is similar to many of their fellow Americans. However, one topic clearly reveals the differences between singlehood in popular America and singlehood in Islam: *sexuality.*

American popular culture encourages and expects single individuals to enjoy a healthy sex life. In contrast, single Muslim young adults too have physical desires, but Islam and culture requires Muslims to refrain from acting on these feelings until marriage. For Muslims who grow up in America - a cultural womb often viewed as sexually "loose" and "lewd" - a tension exists between what is Islamically right and what feels good (temporarily at least) *and* is considered the norm (Haddad and Lummis 1987). We see the old "biological urges vs. cultural suppressions" argument is still a discursive topic in the Muslim community. As one sister declared, *"My body is ready for some babies…. I need to get married asap!"*

Make no mistake; singlehood is not only about sex. But clearly a ban on premarital sex in a society that follows a "new sexual orthodoxy," where sex is a natural right of all, presents a challenge (Moffatt 1989). Still, singlehood is socially constructed, not only through religion but through personal experiences and interactions with the broader culture and members of one's social network, especially family and friends (Gergen in Darrington et al 2005). Just as Islam influences the lives of Muslim young adults, so do college peers, the media, the Internet, music and popular culture.

SO WHAT DID I DO?

With this in mind, I set out to conduct a preliminary investigation. I began to conduct semi-structured qualitative interviews with single young adults of the American Muslim community. In the end, the thirteen women and eight men included in this study range in age from early 20's to mid-30's and represent diverse ethnic and culture backgrounds. All participants self-identify as Muslim, are unmarried and either born and raised in America or spent the majority of their development here. The educational levels ranged from some college to doctoral and professional degrees. Although I originally planned to interview Muslims who live in the Midwest only, mobilizing my network of Muslim friends and employing a system of referrals, took me outside of the Midwest region. These included Muslims who grew up in the Midwest but now live elsewhere, individuals I met at national Muslim conventions, and friends of other interviewees. In the end, my sample included individuals of Arab, Bengali, Black, Latino, Indian, Pakistani, Somalian, and mixed White-Indian heritage. Of these, all were *Sunni* (the largest group of Muslims), except Tariq who is a devout *Shia* (a minority group of Muslims).
Note: All names as well as any identifying information have been changed in order to make the study anonymous.

The Interviews

My interview methodology borrows from life-story interviewing. Chaitin argues that life story interviewers wish "to learn what the individual has lived through, how and where the experiences that the person has had figures into their lives, and how he or she understands life in light of those experiences" (Chaitin 2004:5). A common way to conduct a life-story interview is to provide one simple prompt, "Tell me your life story." My interviews were not quite that open ended, but by leading my informants step-by-step through life experiences, I was able to gain a fuller understanding of their experiences. I also gained insights into the "particular social structures, dynamics and cultural values, morals, and norms in which the individual lives" (Rosenthal in Chaitin 2004:6). Therefore instead of diving right into singlehood proper, interviews generally started with life growing up including K-12 schooling and the ways parents talked about issues such as sexuality, relationships, and life in general. We discussed everything from life in college to the *masjid* and work.

Naturally, every story was unique and interviewees varied in their openness. Some preferred to have more of a dialogue rather than a strict interview in which I alone posed questions. Others simply took a question and ran with it. Either way, in the end, nearly every interviewee, both brothers and sisters stated they enjoyed the opportunity to talk about these issues and reflect on their lives. One interviewee responded, "*It's free therapy ☺.*"

Participant Observation and Review of Cultural Documents

Participant observation is the basis of anthropological research. In addition to the interviews, I visited several *masjids* and Muslim spaces both in my hometowns of Kalamazoo and Detroit, Michigan, as well as around the country. I learned the history of these institutions and participated in rituals and events such as weddings, community dinners and Islamic workshops. I talked with community leaders and other Muslims, male and female, old and young about Muslim singlehood. Two major conferences, MANA (Muslim Alliance of North America) conference and ISNA (Islamic Society of North America) combined with two retreats organized by Seven Shades (an organization for Muslim youth and young adults), provided both access to greater numbers of Muslims, as well as a way to view differences in the organization of Muslim spaces. These trips also helped to place the experiences of my informants on a larger, national scale.

Technology. Technology has extended the realm of Muslim space into cyberworld and in turn, I reviewed Muslim websites like www.altmuslim.com, www.soundvision.com, and www.islamicity.com.

Browsing Muslim matrimonial sites like www.zawaj.com and www.muslimmatch.com, helped to compare the experiences and beliefs of my informants with individuals who anonymously portray their thoughts online. I also found the Muslim blogosphere an interesting site for discourse on Muslim singlehood. Several individuals have taken to writing about singlehood on the internet, as either their entire focus or simply a few influential posts (e.g. www.tariqnelson.com). Lastly, I read Muslim magazines and other publications like Azizah, Muslim Girl, Islamic Horizons and Al Jumah, which often featured useful articles on marriage or Muslim life in America.

Reflections on My Emic Perspective and Style

A researcher's identities and position shape their work and I am no exception. As a 29-year-old married Muslim female who is African-American, I am molded to approach life with particular values and perceptions. For example, this introduction began with my background and experiences as a single *Muslima.* I also included the experiences of friends. Clearly, this influences how I approach Muslim singlehood. I did not come into this research blind and ignorant of Muslim lives and experiences.

I acknowledge I have biases, but my identities also facilitated a smooth entry into this research. First, I am close in age to my participants and people like to talk to people their age right? Second, I'm Muslim. Third, I care about the Muslim community. Ravuvu argues,

> Concern for other's welfare must be the central theme of most researchers if they are to be acceptable and more meaningful to those who are being studied (Ravuvu, 1978:74-76).

All of this helped tremendously in gathering data for this research. I did not really have to "earn" the trust of my informants. I believe most of the Muslims I met saw the study as a benefit to the Muslim community, and thus were willing to support me, either by participating or suggesting a friend. For that, I am thankful.

The Writing

I must admit, gathering the data for this study was the easy part – writing it up was another story. I wanted the text to be useful, both for my discipline and the Muslim community. That meant I needed to find a middle ground. One thing is certain, I wanted to avoid the "dry, analytical prose" that Paul Stoller (1989) argues plagues most anthropological writing. In the *Taste of Ethnographic Things*, he argues,

> Vivid descriptions of the sensorial of ethnographic situations have been largely overshadowed by a dry, analytical prose. In problem-oriented ethnography, data – excluding in large measure the non-visual senses – are used to refine aspects of social theory. Lost on this dry steppe of intellectualized prose are the characterizations of others as they lead their social lives. Such a trend has unfortunately narrowed the readership for most ethnographies, and has made anthropology a discipline in which practitioners increasingly speak only to each other – not to multiple audiences (Stoller 1989:8-9).

Following Stoller's suggestions, I attempt to forge a text that is accessible and engaging. Part of making it accessible is to translate Arabic and Islamic terms. Also because some interviews were conducted online by chat, I often spell out commonly used abbreviations like "lol" for laughing out loud, "iA" for *InshaAllah* (God Willing), "lmao" for laughing my a*@ off, "brb" for be right back, "u" for you, "k" for ok, and "esp" for "especially". I include a glossary of Arabic and Internet chat phrases used within the book.

Some who are not accustomed to parenthetical citations may find them difficult to ignore – this is something I hope to change in the second edition. Lastly, please note that I often adopt the popular tendency to refer to Muslim men as "brothers" and Muslim women as "sisters." I use the term *masjid* to refer to mosque - the two terms are synonymous. I also use the popular term *desi* to refer to South Asian Americans.

INSIDE THE BOOK

Following this introduction, the book is divided into three parts:

Part I: Background includes Chapter 1: *Identities, Youth and American Muslims*, which focuses on identity construction, youth culture and ethnographies concerning American life as well as religious minorities. I explore notions of the "third space," a place where individuals hybridize and negotiate plural identities. Chapter 2: *The Cultural Wombs That Bore Us*, offers a synthesis of influences shaping the identities, worldviews, beliefs, behaviors and meanings of singlehood for Muslim young adults. The discussion centers on aspects of Islam, American pluralism, individualism and popular culture, and family and ethnicity.

Part II: Eight Reasons Muslim Singlehood is Hard (Chapters 3-10), presents ethnographic data highlighting specific challenges facing Muslim young adults. The discussion includes levels of religious identification, loneliness, desires for intimacy and difficulties finding a spouse.

Part III: Conclusions includes Chapter 11, *Easing the Singlehood Path*, which offers suggestions for the Muslim community to address the issues raised in Part II. These include increasing dialogue around issues of singlehood, reducing the stigma on singles, exploring new ways of courting, and having help from *masjids*. Lastly, Chapter 12 provides a summary and final thoughts.

The **Appendices** include *On the Journey to Marriage* – A Practical Guide for preparing for marriage; *A Letter to the Brothers* by Halim Naeem, and a sample of *So You Wanna Know* ™, a fun game couples, families and communities can use to get to know one another.

PART I

BACKGROUND

1

Identities, Youth and American Muslims

You now know *why* I conducted this study, as well as *how* I conducted this study. What's needed now is to understand a bit more about *who* was studied. American Muslims are just one of several groups of minorities in America, a pluralistic society. So what have scholars said about constructing identity in a place with so many different ways of living? And how do youth and young adults contribute to change in society?

This chapter examines some of the literature that answers these questions as well as a few studies of American Muslims' negotiation of competing ideologies. My goal is to lay the foundation for understanding the complex lived experiences of America Muslim young adults; including various competing cultural wombs (discussed in Chapter 2) and the challenges of singlehood (discussed in chapters 3-10).

Identity

If you're anything like me, your email gets bombarded with spam and meaningless forwards from friends. The bulk simply ends up in the trash folder, but one video caught my eye: "Is it really possible to be both a Texan and a Muslim?" asked a Dallas news broadcaster. The news report titled, *Turning Muslim in Texas* chronicled the lives of three white Texan converts to Islam and posed this question to mostly white Americans in Texas. Responses ranged from "*Hmm, I don't know. That would be a weird combination*" to "*I'm not sure. What do they believe, do they believe in God?*"

In the age of digital editing, it is very probable the producers removed the "*Yes*" responses to achieve a stronger piece of journalism. Nevertheless, at the base of this video are clear ideas about what it means to be a "Muslim" and what it means to be a "Texan," or more broadly, what it means to be an "American." The responses given imply that many average Americans feel there is a line of difference between a Muslim religious identity and an American national identity - and that line precludes any sort of compatibility.

America is clearly a mosaic comprised of individuals hailing from a variety of religious and ethnic backgrounds. Why does this type of newscast exist in a pluralistic society? Well, one of the interesting side effects of multiculturalism is that individuals often see themselves forming an insular group, distinct from other groups. Though they recognize the multi-dimensional nature of identity (e.g. I'm a male white Catholic American), many continue to treat the idea as fixed and one-dimensional (Khan 2000). They view their identity along lines of sameness and group cohesiveness, something Stuart Hall, an influential theorist, sees as "a sort of collective one true self " (S. Hall 1990:223).

This type of view can give authority and legitimacy to visions of community, but can also strengthen stereotypes about communities (Khan 2000). The idea of a "Muslim" identity and an "American" identity put forth in the above story is a vivid example this occurrence. But when individuals bind together through shared history and collective characteristics, they often form what Anderson (1991) calls an *imagined community*. He argues that a nation,

> is imagined because the members of even the smallest nation will never know most of their fellow-members, meet them, or even hear of them, yet in the minds of each lives the image of their communion … regardless of the actual inequality and exploitation that may prevail in each, the nation is always conceived as a deep, horizontal comradeship (Anderson 1991:6-7).

This observation of a national identity extends to other types of identities, whether religious, ethnic, racial, gender or socio-economic. Though the *feeling* of belonging exists, it is simply impractical to expect all members of *any* group to enact their identity in the same way.

Given the nature of an *imagined community,* it is understandable that many Americans have clear ideas about true "American ideals" - which is of course what formed the premise of the newscaster's question. Why would someone treat a Muslim identity, which is simply a religious identity, along the same lines as a more encompassing national identity? I will touch on Islamophobia later, but I first want to explore the perceived "American" ideals and why this is important in a study on Muslim singlehood.

Being American

Huntington (2004) argues that an American identity is not based on ethnic or race values, but on a culture and creed left by the Anglo-Protestant founders of the country. Key elements of which include, "the English language; Christianity; religious commitment; English concepts of the rule of law, including the responsibility of rulers and the rights of individuals; and dissenting Protestant values of individualism, the work ethic, and the belief that humans have the ability and the duty to try to create a heaven on earth, a 'city on a hill' " (Huntington 2004:xvi). Huntington maintains this creed has remained stable over time, however, this widely accepted depiction of "American" culture is overly simplistic of the array of ideals found amongst Americans.

Contemporary theorists reject identity as one-dimensional and instead situate it as plural, fluid, dynamic and heterogeneous (those interested can see the works of S. Hall 1990, 1992, 1996, Bhabha 1994, Brah 1996, Sokefeld 1999, K. Hall 2002, Khan 2000). Individuals simultaneously possess a number of identities, and have the ability to identify with several communities at once. A quick example is Brah, a "Ugandan of Indian descent," who examines the complexity of identity and argues that naming a singular identity would render invisible "all the other identities – of gender, caste, religion, linguistic group, generation…" (Brah 1996:3). She sees her identities as meshing and incapable of complete separation.

So we see, living in a pluralistic society allows an individual the opportunity to create and re-create their version of reality based on their interpretation of, and interactions with the several competing ideologies and worldviews they encounter on a daily basis (K. Hall 2005:473). These competing ideologies set in motion, the construction of identities (religious, national and ethnic) along lines of internal difference as S. Hall writes, "in modern times, (identities are) increasingly fragmented and fractured; never singular but multiply constructed across different, often intersecting and antagonistic, discourses, practices and positions" (S. Hall 1996:4).

Being American Muslim

To illustrate this idea, S. Hall and other theorists often utilize Jacques Derrida's concept of *différance* (see Sokefeld 1999, Ewing 1998, Bhabha 1994, Brah 1996). Derrida, a linguist, points to two meanings of the Latin verb *differre*: "to differ" and "to defer," that is, "to cause delay," "to temporize," and "to dislocate." The first meaning, "to differ" is straightforward. However, the second meaning, "to temporize" acknowledges that *différance* is continuously moving and modified (Sokefeld 1999). Applied to identity, *différance* indicates that the meanings of identity are not only in flux, but because they relate to each other, identities they will always be created and recreated.

Muslim American identities, like all identities are plural. We must debunk the myth that all Muslims think, dress, eat and drink alike.

This is one of the reasons we must first explore identity in order to understand the lives of American Muslims and their singlehood. With Muslims, there is a sense of *différance* vis-à-vis the dominant culture - Muslims are an American religious minority and *different* from the Christian majority. But secondly, we acknowledge that within the American Muslim community there are *several* lines of *différance* drawn upon generational, racial, ethnic and class differences. The American Muslim community does not constitute a homogeneous group. The question becomes, how do individuals achieve internal balance when these plural identities often include competing values and discourses? For this discussion, we turn to hybridity and the "third space."

Hybridity and Identity Politics

Muslims live in a pluralistic society, which often means that they belong to two or more distinct cultural groups simultaneously, e.g. Muslims of South Asian descent or Muslim college students. Naturally, each of these groups has their own "norms." As people encounter contradictory cultural wombs, they embrace or reject the cultural influences that play at the "parameters of their conscious awareness" (K.Hall 2002:194). Adopting those things that are familiar and comfortable, and rejecting that which is too foreign.

Social acceptance is a natural desire of humankind

Bhabha's notion of *hybridity* in the "third space", a sort of identity interstice or middle ground, is a useful tool to understand the process of blending two or more identities.

> It is in the emergence of the interstices--the overlap and displacement of domains of difference -- that the intersubjective and collective experiences of nationness, community interest, or cultural value are negotiated. How are subjects formed 'in-between', or in excess of, the sum of the 'parts' of difference (usually intoned as race/class/gender, etc.)? How do strategies of representation or empowerment come to be formulated in the competing claims of communities where, despite shared histories of deprivation and discrimination, the exchange of values, meanings and priorities may not always be collaborative and dialogical, but may be profoundly antagonistic, conflictual and even incommensurable (Bhabha 1994:2)?

As my father would joke, "*That's some PhD talk – totally incomprehensible!*" However, Bhabha raises an important point, when individuals negotiate identities they engage the greater community.

Id includes oth.

Identities are performed not only for self, but for others (Madison 2005). Identity negotiation becomes a political process with individuals exerting strategic moves to achieve more power.

This "power" does not have to be economic. It can include the more subdued clout that comes with social acceptance. Remember the popular kid in school and how everyone looked up to them? To achieve that feeling, individuals may engage in behavior that runs contradictory to what they feel is their "core" identity. Receiving positive societal feedback and a sense of belonging and peace becomes more important. Think for a moment about how this may affect the lives of single Muslims, the stories in Part II are examples.

Brah argues that this desire for security and belonging is innate. When a performed identity is not accepted, or worse - devalued, not only is the individual's sense of peace disrupted, but it often brings on a struggle for power. Here, Kondo vividly illustrates how identity flux, boundaries, hybridity and power are sometimes engaged.

> Power can create identities on the individual level, as it provides disciplines, punishments, and culturally available pathways for fulfillment; nowhere were these forces more evident to me than in my relationships with the Japanese people I knew. At stake in my narrative of emerging order are the constantly contested and shifting boundaries of my identity and the identities of my Japanese relatives friends, and acquaintances… in that attempt to understand (each other), power inevitably came into play as we tried to force each other into appropriately comprehensible categories. This nexus of power and meaning was also creative, the crucible within which we forged our relationship. In turn, our negotiated understandings of one another enabled me to shape the particular problematic that now animates my research. The sites of these struggles for understanding were located in what we might call salient features of "identity" both in America and in Japan: race, gender, and age (Kondo 1990:10-11).

Both Kondo and her Japanese relatives held clear ideas about what it means to be Japanese; and they both struggled to make their version of reality appealing to the other.

Likewise, communities, nations and other groups of individuals have clear ideas about how to perform the feature they feel sets their identity apart, whether it be race/ethnicity, gender, age or religion, etc. This type of power struggle often occurs between members of the younger and older generation. Youth and young adults (I include individuals up to 40), more than any other group, live in the "third space" where they are both more open to outside influences and in a position to bring about great changes. The next section looks at theories of youth culture, which reveal ways young people produce cultural change.

YOUNG PEOPLE CHANGE SOCIETY

Parents and community are the first to model and mold children's identities, but soon age and life experiences reveal an *infinite* number of possible identities (Adamson and Lyxell 1996). As a result, studying youth (individuals under the age of 35-40), and their negotiation of competing ideologies (and construction of hybrid identities), reveals a wide range of social issues. It also provides a unique lens for understanding the creativity of culture, and the texture of cultural change (Halperin and Scheld 2007).

A lot of people like to see youth as mere inhabitants of a liminal stage on their way to full adulthood, that they are not important until they come into full leadership. Wulff (1993) argues that neglecting to view youth as "cultural agents" can mean missing out on learning about new society trends. When youth negotiate conflicting messages and create a hybrid identity, they bring about new cultural meaning which affects not only themselves, but society as a whole (Bhabha 1994:227; Bucholtz 2002).

See for example, the life experiences of British Sikh youth who understand, internalize and shape the racial, social and ethnic inequalities they face (K.Hall 2002). More and more of these youth achieved social mobility by "knowing when to act English and when to act Indian." It is unfortunate that this process was necessary at all, but these youth made conscious decisions to "be successful, challenge inequality, and find a bit of happiness in their everyday lives" (K.Hall 2002:195).

The same goes for Muslim young adults, second and third generation immigrants as well as indigenous Muslims who are working through identity conflicts (Leonard 2003). Living in a non-Muslim society where common practices such as dating and premarital sex, drug and alcohol use permeate (but are strictly forbidden in Islam), provides a challenge for Muslims who wish to maintain religious values and lifestyles. Again, in a pluralistic society which hails multiculturalism, this struggle is often more internal than external (Moore 2007). Yet pluralism does not expunge social pressures (e.g. peer pressure, family influences, media, lacks of accommodation, etc.) that may cause one to question their version of reality, and their Islamic identity.

Islamic Anchor

To cope, many Muslims use Islam as an identity anchor. Investigating the relationship between multiculturalism and identity amongst British Muslims, Gilliat-Ray argues that young Muslims find the 'core' of Islam and construct religious identities centered on their faith (Gilliat-Ray 1998). This helps them deal with differences in "selfhood" between themselves, born and raised in Britain, and the first generation of Muslim immigrants. Studies of American youth also document this trend (see Grewal 2008, Yip 2006).

Studying youth and young adults reveals large cultural trends and directions in cultural change

Likewise, Zine (2001) explores the connection between religion and other sites of social difference like race, gender and language amongst "practicing" Muslim youth in Canadian schools. She places their struggle for a hybrid identity within three, often conflicting cultural frameworks: the dominant culture, their ethnic culture and Islam. For these students, adopting a religious identification and joining other Muslim students anchored their sense of identity. Islam also provided a framework to preserve students' lifestyles and resist unwanted social pressures (e.g. negative peer pressure, gender interaction, racism and discrimination).

Another study by Mir (2006), argues that the dialectical relationship between Muslim women and the dominant peer culture forces Muslim women into the "third space" to overcome marginality and construct their identities. Relevant to this study are the young women's rules pertaining to gender relationships. Many were shocked at college culture's sexual nature that normalized and even Americanized dating.

Muslim women who did not date were often interrogated by their peers. To resist the pressure to date and have sex, some young Muslim women preferred Muslim-only circles. Those who did not separate themselves from non-Muslims often felt "left out because romance and sex were such essential elements to the (college) lifestyle" (Mir 2006:226). Resistance and hybridization were daily activities.

CHAPTER SUMMARY

We see that Muslim identities, like all identities are not one-dimensional static concepts. They are dynamic and constructed along lines of difference within specific historical and cultural settings (S. Hall 1990). The current cultural settings present several competing ideologies and worldviews, which American Muslims internalize and hybridize in the *third space,* a liminal site of identity construction. No two Muslims conduct this process equally, and thus the American Muslim community is diverse and heterogeneous in its views. By extension, Muslim singlehood is diverse and heterogeneous. This book does not present a cookie-cutter version of Muslim singlehood but instead aims to reveal the multifaceted nature of the reality.

This chapter also provided a brief analysis of youth culture, in particular, how studying youth can reveal social issues and modes of cultural change. Lastly, we have seen the ways some young Muslims use Islam as a religious anchor.

Having now provided a framework for interpreting the lives of single Muslims, the next chapter contributes by examining three competing ideologies, what I term cultural wombs, which single Muslim young adults encounter on a daily basis.

2

THE CULTURAL WOMBS THAT BORE US

O mankind! Reverence your Guardian Lord who created you from a single person, and created, of like nature, his mate, and from them twain scattered (like seeds) countless men and women. Reverence God through Whom you demand (mutual) rights. And (reverence) the wombs (that bore you): for God ever watches over you. (Quran 4:1)

I remember attending a few Muslim weddings where my father, the *Imam* (officiate), would use this Quranic verse to illustrate that each individual is born within certain circumstances and conditions. Though the most obvious interpretation of "Reverence the wombs that bore you," would be to respect your mother and the biological womb that endured pregnancy and birth, he suggested there are several "*wombs*" that nurture human beings. For some reason, that has always resonated with me and I often use it to think about the influences in my life.

By extension, a *cultural womb* is a place/field/space that cultivates and nourishes human development while preparing individuals for life outside of its borders. As the physical womb develops a child with or without the mother's agency, the socially regulated cultural womb can also instill particular behaviors, beliefs, and emotions - with or without an individual's knowledge or assistance.

I realize that the term "womb" brings with it several meanings. Some will see it as purely insular in nature, incapable of interacting with other "wombs." Others may see it as a "nurturing" place and by extension not be able to connect it to aspects of culture that are not nurturing. Stuart Hall and Bhabha think of this same idea as each identity having a boundary (there is a line you cross – the third space being the space between two identities). Others prefer the term "cultural fields." My preference for "cultural wombs" is simply personal in nature, but I acknowledge that others may prefer to use other terms.

Kathleen Hall, who prefers "cultural fields," highlights the regulatory process conducted within a cultural womb.

> The regularities of routine practices in a cultural field both reproduce and create cultural expectations for bodily gestures and dress, for appropriate manners and signs of respect between generations and the sexes, and for the cultural knowledge people use to interpret social interactions (K.Hall 2002:171).

Routine practices become customs, and customs become what Durkheim (1938) termed 'social facts', or simply the natural order of things. In the words of Butler, this "performativity", the process through which "regulatory schemas or ideals condition social practice over time and norms are 'assumed, appropriated, taken on'," is important to acknowledge when examining the hows and whys behind individual actions (Butler in K.Hall 2002:171).

In this light, this chapter highlights the ideals and norms of three large, overarching *cultural wombs*: Islam, America, and ethnic and family networks. Each of these organizes social life through cultural competences and normative expectations. In particular, I pay attention to each wombs' practices and beliefs that regulate or influence the interactions between single Muslim young adults as well as their views of marriage and singlehood, mate selection, and the conceptions of being "good" and "normal."

WOMB #1: ISLAM

On one *Jumah* Friday, the day of Muslims' prayer service, I sat on the carpeted floor of the *musala* (prayer hall) listening to the *khutbah* (sermon) with about 15 other sisters. The day's topic centered on using Islam to repair social ills. The Imam stated, "*Islam is the answer to all our problems, all we have to do is apply it.*" In order for this to be realistic, Islamic principles must be quite extensive, and certainly, scholars have written volumes on just one small aspect of Islam. Obviously, I am no Islamic scholar. My goal here is not to conduct a thorough reading of Islamic theology, but rather to highlight some of the key doctrines that contribute to a single Muslim's religious identity.

The Quran & Prophet Muhammad

Muslims believe the Quran, a compilation book of revelations received by Prophet Muhammad, ranks as the highest source of moral guidance. They study it for direction on everything from legal matters, to orphan care, inheritance, and of course, sex and marriage. In regards to singlehood, the Quran highly regards family, and encourages Muslims to marry if possible.

> O Humans revere your Guardian Lord, Who created you from a single person and created of like nature its mate, and from this scattered (like seeds) countless men and women... (Quran 4:1).
>
> And among His signs is this, that He created for you mates from among yourselves, that you may dwell in peace and tranquility with them, and He has put love and mercy between your (hearts). Verily in that are signs for those who reflect (Quran 30:21).

If we think back for a moment to the literature cited earlier, the studies of Stein (1975) and DePaulo (2006) who argue American marriage is on the decline – we can see that for Muslims this is not the case. While long-term singlehood is not forbidden, marriage is certainly introduced as the ideal institution to bring peace and love to humankind. It is also the only way to enjoy sexual activity - the Quran prohibits extramarital sex and praises chastity (see Quran 17:32; 33:35). Sex is seen as natural and innate, but also as a gift to be enjoyed within marriage only. To protect themselves from sexual temptation, many Muslims also ban activities that *may* lead to sex, like kissing or being alone with someone of the opposite sex.

If it wasn't for hell, singlehood would probably be a bit easier!

Following the Quran, the second source of guidance is the *hadith*, the reliably transmitted reports of what the Prophet said or did. *Note: After the Prophet's name, Muslims invoke a short prayer, "peace be upon him". I shall adopt that in this text and shorten it to 'pbuh'.* Informants often quoted *hadith* that exalt marriage like, "Marriage is half of your religion, so fear Allah with the other half" or "Marriage is my way, whoever does not marry is not of my people" (Bukhari & Muslim).

Muslims see marriage as a shield from promiscuity, adultery and fornication, which most feel leads to the disintegration of family and community. Likewise, informants recalled *hadith* like, "when a man and woman are alone together, Satan is the third," to support their views of gender separation.

While many quote the *hadith* verbatim, some may simply generalize a saying to lend extra credence to their argument. For example, Grewal (2008) quotes a parent that guesses at a *hadith* to justify racial endogamy.

> I tell my daughters that I think it's easier to marry within similar backgrounds. *And I can't quote you a hadith [Prophetic tradition] but I know there is one that says try to marry within similar backgrounds, just to avoid conflict because,* as [it] is, there are too many difference in the marriage. That is why we parents say stay in your own race background. (Grewal 2008:15-16, *emphasis added*).

Herein lies what many informants saw as the danger of *hadith* – Muslims' reference to them without understanding the context in which they were used. Most accepted and appreciated the hadith, but did not like when they were used to enforce or criminalize behaviors without knowing the context of the statements.

Living as a Muslim

prac·tice

1. To do or perform habitually or customarily; make a habit of: practices courtesy in social situations.
2. To do or perform (something) repeatedly in order to acquire or polish a skill: practice a dance step.
3. To give lessons or repeated instructions to; drill: practiced the students in handwriting.
4. To work at, especially as a profession: practice law.
5. To carry out in action; observe: practices a religion piously.

What does it mean to "practice" Islam? When Muslims refer to the word "practice," they are often measuring one's commitment to Islam, otherwise known as Islamic religiosity. See, for example, Nailah's response when I asked if her family was "religious."

> I don't know. I never understood the concept of being religious when I was younger. I thought either you practiced or you didn't. We practiced. My dad taught us how to pray, taught us about Allah, read us Quran at night, stories about the prophet, etc…

Thus the question, "Is s/he a *practicing* Muslim or a *cultural* Muslim?" popularly refers to whether someone is a Muslim in deed, or in speech. And at a base level, "in deed" includes an adherence to the five pillars of Islam:

Shahadah	to state belief in One God and the prophethood of Muhammad
Salat	to pray five prayers each day
Sawm	to fast from dawn to sunset during the month of *Ramadan* each year
Zakat	to pay charity each year

Hajj	to make the pilgrimage to Makkah once in a lifetime

At a minimum, Muslims are expected to adhere to these pillars, but several actions extend beyond the five pillars - including a faith in the afterlife.

The Afterlife

Muslims believe in heaven, hell, and a day of judgment in which one's fate in the next life will be determined based on actions on earth. As we saw during my husband search, this belief can affect an individual's attitudes *and* behaviors. In my case, the stronger I focused on the afterlife, the less likely I was to do anything I deemed "un-Islamic." Actions take on a deeper meaning for someone who sees life on earth as merely a *part* of human existence.

One sister exclaimed, *"If it wasn't for hell, singlehood would probably be a blast. Dating, one-night stands, hanging out…I could do whatever I want!"* (This person would benefit from Frietas' book titled *Sex and the Soul.* Though that lifestyle may seem appealing, Frietas found that many college students are unsatisfied participants). But for many Muslims, every action is accompanied by the question: "Does this get me closer or farther from my goal of *Jannah* (heaven)?"

Believing in Heaven and Hell can certainly affect whether you decide to take that cute man or woman up on their offer.

Yet Muslims do not always internalize or enact the above beliefs/practices in the same way. For example, one Muslim sister who is much more liberal in her views declared, *"Do you think I don't have sex because I'm thinking about hell? (laughing) You've got to be kidding. Most people choose to have or not have sex because of pregnancy and diseases, not because of Hell."*

You will find Muslims who drink (though Islam prohibits alcohol), Muslims who smoke (though Islam prohibits intoxicants) and Muslims who have premarital sex (though Islam prohibits sex outside of marriage). One sister explains,

> I know people who hardly pray, or struggle with their prayers, or don't even seem to try to struggle but they fast, and cover (*hijab*) and eat *halal* (Meat from animals

> slaughtered with the Name of God). Or they pray (struggle), fast but don't cover and believe. .. then there are people who pray, fast, believe and have sex. Not married. (Nailah, 28)

These Muslims are commonly referred to as "cultural" Muslims. So why the variation? The fact is, Muslims are simply human beings. When pushed into the third space, they negotiate the contradictions in relation to their religiosity, beliefs and desires, and choose for themselves which parts of Islam to engage.

Still when conflicts between individual and collective identities occur, collectively most Muslims desire for "Muslim" to be the most salient identity.

I'm Muslim First

In *Bilal's Stand*, a film by Sultan Sharieff about a Black Muslim teenager struggling to maintain his Islamic identity, the lead character Bilal is at a party with friends when a few girls approach, grab his arm and lead him to the dance floor. Reflecting on what his classmates would think if he did not "allow her to grind up on me," Bilal states, *"Parties are what I call splitters, yea see here you're not able to be a Muslim and a teenager at the same time. You gotta split your personality in order to survive."* Bilal desired the sense of social belonging discussed earlier by Brah (1996).

Others would disagree with Bilal and suggest that you can never "split" away from your Muslim identity. They would suggest that Bilal should not have gone to the "un-Islamic" party in the first place, that he should have been "Muslim First" (Naber 2005).

Several studies like Naber's study of Arab American Muslims argue that the current social context (of multiculturalism and pluralism) has brought about the emergence of "Muslim First" as a possible collective identity (Naber 2005:479). Grewal (2008) also noted this trend amongst South Asian and Arab second-generation youth, Karim (2005) amongst African-American young adults and Naguib (2003) amongst young European Muslims. Fatima, a Pakistani American sister in this study concurs,

> I'm Muslim first. So there are things that I can't do that are normal here: drink, dance with guys, have sex. After that

> there are things in the American culture that if they don't' contradict any religious beliefs I can adapt. That's how I think about the American culture. And the South Asian culture? Same thing. I'm Muslim first, if there are things in my culture that aren't Islamic I can challenge them (like the idea of women being your chef and laundry maid ☺)

As Fatima hinted, it's not just Islamic identities but American and ethnic identities that play a part in decision making. For her, filtering out those aspects of life that do not conform to Islam is an easy process.

WOMB #2: AMERICA
LAND OF FREEDOM, SEX AND POLITICS

Individualism

There is a song by Mick Jagger that says, "I'm Free to do what I want any ole time!" In American culture, decisions are mostly made for the comfort of the individual, not one's kin, society or religion (Schnieder 1968). However, prior to the 1950s, American individualism focused mainly on the political domain - freedom of religion, freedom of speech, freedom to choose our own place of residence (Yankelovich 1998). During the 1960s, individualism broadened from politics to personal lifestyles. Individuals could express their talents, sexuality, dress, and other likes and dislikes without fear of being labeled a social outcast. This trend continued into the 1970s and led journalist Tom Wolfe to go so far as to label the young adults of the time the "Me Generation" (Twenge 2006).

Today, some 40 years later, individualism is still a major part of American culture and certainly influences the meaning of American Muslim singlehood. For example, in discussing her sexuality in *On the Edge of Becoming* a chapter in *Living Islam Out Loud*, Khalida Saed, a lesbian Muslim wrote, "I'm not sure I would have had the balls to discuss my sexuality at all, or even consider it, if my American side hadn't told me I had the right" (Saed in Ghafur 2005:86).

In another way, individualism influences the decision of marriage or not. Stein found individuals who chose to stay single and saw marriage as "an entrapment, requiring constant accommodation and compromise and cutting off variety of experience" (Stein 1975:490). As one informant explained,

> There aren't any conditions under which I would consider getting married.....I want freedom of choice, freedom to do what I want instead of being tied to living with just one person and doing the same, mutually satisfying, things over and over (Stein 1975:494).

Individualism, Popular Sex Culture and Islamophobia all contribute to Muslims' attitudes and behaviors

For Muslims, individualism plays more into spousal selection and delay of marriage more so than out right rejection. It also plays into religiosity. Several brothers and sisters cited their desire to "choose my way (my religion) for myself." *Note that the Quran also states religion is an individual's personal choice.* When informants participated in activities that diverge either from Islamic or parental teachings, they felt it was their personal right to decide their own life course, an idea discussed further in chapter three.

Though supposedly individualistic, someone coming to America for the first time may be surprised at just how much popular culture advises individuals on everything from how to dress, what to eat, what car to drive, what color to paint your room, what centerpiece to use for a wedding, and of course, how to date and get married. In actuality, many decisions are in reference to these prescripts which then come to be seen as an individual's "choice." Thus again, we return to the notion of cultural "womb" which often acts on an individual with or without their cognitive agency.

The Glamorization of Sex

I don't have to tell you that sex is everywhere. From "sensually smooth chocolate bars" to primetime sex scenes, sexual acts have crept into nearly every aspect of American life. As a result, while Muslims (of all backgrounds) enjoy and appreciate the freedoms of America, many view mainstream American society as one of "loose" values and "lewd" behavior (Haddad and Lummis 1987).

Take for example the sexually explicit songs played on popular radio stations. Nadirah, 21, revealed, *"I am serious I don't even listen to rap anymore really because of that mess. All they talk about is sex and how good it is on every song (laughing). It's true, all I hear is sex, drugs and GET MONEY on every song!"*

Some songs like Mariah Carey's *Touch my Body*, not only normalize sexual behavior but even go as far to label it "American." *WARNING: Sexually Explicit lyrics!*

Touch my body
Put me on the floor
Wrestle me around
Play with me some more
Touch my body
Throw me on the bed
I just wanna make you feel
Like you never did.
Touch my body
Let me wrap my thighs
All around your waist
Just a little taste
Touch my body
Know you love my curves
Come on and give me what I deserve
And touch my body …

The remix lyrics with R.Kelly:

Oh yes indeed
It's the **American dream**
When I touch yo
Work yo, taste yo body
I want you to do to my

Get up on my
Sit up on my body…

Meeting a stranger for sex is the "American Dream?" These songs directly contradict Islamic teachings by glamorizing sexual behavior (without commitment). Through their enticing beats (I have a love-hate relationship with this song), they appeal and influence the masses. However, music is not alone. These sexual messages also fill nearly 60% of television programs (Fisherkeller 1997), and influence the sexual behaviors of youth and young adults (Collins et al 2006; Aubrey et al 2003; Fisherkeller 1997). Jaydeb, a Bengali-American remarked that television was one of the first things his parents began to monitor when he arrived to America at age 10. He said, *"They said I couldn't watch it because it would teach me bad stuff, I think they were right (laughing)."*

Perhaps the type of "bad stuff" Jaydeb's parents were referring to is the type of activity filling the storylines of popular TV shows like *Desperate Housewives.* For example, a few of the main characters contract and spread a sexually transmitted disease. One character, is married but is also having an affair with her ex-husband, whom she previously cheated on with her underage gardener. A pregnant teenage girl is sent away while her mother pretends to be pregnant herself in order to preserve her standing in the community. Lastly, during Susan's pregnancy, a teenage boy mistakes her new larger breasts for implants (and she for a stripper). When she corrects him, he replies, "That's hot." (Adopted from www.parentstv.org)

Perhaps Jaydeb's parents were concerned about the soft pornography music videos shown on MTV, BET and VH1 where men and scantly dressed women simulate sexual positions. Or maybe it was the television advertisements like for Victoria's Secrets, Viagra, AXE deodorant spray, cologne and even shampoo, contain sexual innuendos. Or I suppose it could have been other depictions of singlehood like "The Bachelor," where several women compete for the "love" of one man or and "Hell Date" where paid actors trick and terrorize their dates. Both shows send negative messages about relationships, commitment and the bases of marriage. Or finally, they could have been concerned about the most popular shows about singlehood like *Sex and the City.* The main characters often had one-night stands and other frivolous relationships. I think you get my point, as one brother said, *"sex is everywhere, you can't escape it!"*

Sex and College Life

Naturally, popular culture's glamorization of sex carries into the lives of college students. *Coming of Age in New Jersey*, an ethnography about college culture, highlights the complexity of sexual and intimate relationships (Moffatt 1989). Following parental values and religious upbringings, Moffatt found contemporary American culture to be the major influence on college student's sexualities; students were drawn to sex from an early age. He also rediscovers Heath's (1982) notion of a "new sexual orthodoxy" where sex is viewed as an important and normal human right and "central to one's sense of self" (Moffatt 1989:195). Even most of the students who were virgins desired sex and were ashamed of their virginity. One student wrote,

> I have never had sexual contact of any kind: no intercourse, no petting, no kissing, no anything. And I am not proud of this fact. You see, I am shy.. [but] I am not a prude; I'm not content with my lifestyle. I believe in premarital sex; I just haven't been fortunate enough to have any. I consider sex a basic need in life, comparable to food and shelter. – Junior male. (Moffatt 1989:195)

Similarly, Holland and Eisenhart (1990) find the sexual peer culture of many colleges to be saturated with a "cultural model of romance and attractiveness" (106). Two-thirds of the college women they studied spent much of their time proving their attractiveness to men, hoping to achieve a relationship. Those who received attention from males in the form of gifts, phone calls or sexual advances from men, were most admired by friends and roommates.

The authors suggest that this sex culture sets up college women to be "mobbed by romance" and placed on the "sexual auction block." Universities themselves are also to blame. Campus sponsored events like mixers, presume an interest in finding a boyfriend and create a culture where romance is coveted. The authors use this to highlight the failure of the universities in protecting these women from a sexualized college culture.

While the college women could not completely evade gender relations, some women devised culturally acceptable strategies to escape the "sexual auction block." For example, keeping an absentee or workaholic boyfriend could be useful to avoid unwanted invitations from other men on campus. Black women employed self-reliance as a resistance strategy, stating that they did not need a man to furnish their needs - something the authors suggest may be due to the low-economic status of many men within the black community although I did not experience this on my college campus.

Many Muslims would fall into the categories above, some have equally devised modes of resistance. Some informants simply limited relationships to escape the pulls of sex. Nailah who believes her religious background and parents' teachings "protected" her from "undesirable activities" states,

> I mean in college there was more at stake, the three letter word. I had my own space, no one could tell me anything. I could have sex if I wanted to, so to avoid that, no boyfriends. I realize that at an older age sex is generally expected or desired in a relationship.

The other side of this are the brothers. If women are working to prove their attractiveness to men, the men are the recipients of such flirtation. Several brothers in this study recounted being chased by "girls" and how the peer culture rewards the guys who "had a lot of girls" or "could prove they had sex." For those who chose not to engage in these types of activities, it became a challenge to maintaining their "manhood" without engaging in the sex culture. (*The Appendix: "A letter to the Brothers" by Halim Naeem addresses this from a brothers perspective).*

Religion, College and Sex

How does religion factor in? Though sexual activity is the norm, students with a strong sense of religiosity tend to be less sexually active and are more likely to hold conservative attitudes regarding premarital sex, use abstinence or withdrawal as a means of contraception (Beckwith and Morrow 2005). Less religious students tend to hold more "sexually permissive attitudes, less conventional values, and less traditional values or roles regarding sex or sexual behavior" (Beckwith and Morrow 2005: 357-367).

Returning to Moffatt's (1989) study, only three of his 144 participants self identified as "intentional virgins." All three were women and all three were Catholics who saw their virginity as a personal decision.

> I don't consider myself a prude, but I strongly believe that for me sex without commitment (marriage) is wrong. I stress "for me" because although I feel that my morals are right, I generally don't judge other people. – senior female (Moffatt 1989:196)

Interestingly, of the sexually active students, 20% expressed some form of sexual guilt that Moffat attributes to their Roman Catholic background.

> All in all I feel my sexual experiences were very enjoyable.... Sometimes I feel a little guilty about sex – caused by my up-bringing and my religious beliefs. I sometimes have the urge to confess about my "pre-marital sexual experiences" to a priest and give up these experiences until married, but I realize that I am too tempted to ever commit myself against indulging in such activities. - Senior female (Moffatt 1989:203)

This leads me to Freitas (2008) who studies the intersection between religious identities and the sexual attitudes/behaviors of college students. Freitas discovers that most evangelical Christian college students are virgins, or at least strive to have a commitment to abstinence, while "secular" students tend to be more sexually experienced. However, the most interesting finding for me was though students were active participants in the campuses' sexual peer culture, they often found sex "unsatisfying" and longed for more "meaningful" relationships. As one student explains,

> We're not happy with the hookup culture.... We feel a constant pressure to do things that make us feel unsettled. We want meaningful relationships that integrate spirituality (whatever that turns out to be) into our dating lives (whatever that turns out to mean) (Freitas 2008:xiv).

Frietas states,

> They wanted the right to demand more from their peers when it came to sex and relationships – more joy, more satisfaction, more commitment- and less sex. Maybe even no sex (Freitas 2008:xiv).

The students at evangelical and secular colleges had different college experiences but they were alike in many ways. Both felt religious and/or spiritual identities are important. They all desire sex and long to act on that desire but often feel sex is not necessary for romance. Reconciling sex and the soul was a struggle and students experience a great degree of shame, regret or angst with regard to sex. Lastly, students do not know where to turn to for advice (adopted from Frietas 2008:215-216). Hmm, sounds familiar!

Many college students involved in the peer sexual culture long for more meaningful relationships

The study is an important contribution to literature on college students and religion, but Freitas' failure to include Muslim perspectives is disappointing. In addition to evangelical Christianity, Frietas included brief looks at Judaism and Buddhism, but not Islam. This study reveals that Muslims have much in common with both the evangelical as well as "secular" students. Muslims who are more religiously conservative tend to be more concerned with monitoring their sexual behaviors and more in line with the evangelical students. These types of people were the majority of those I studied. Interestingly, those Muslims who "explore" life as a "secular" student, like those of Freitas' study, often in the end find it unsatisfying. After exploring, many return to life as a "Muslim" in the end, usually when they are in more of a marriage mindset.

It is also interesting that many brothers and sisters in this study (similar to peer pressure), were concerned about maintaining a good reputation (in the Muslim community). The Muslim communities are still very small and definitely have their own brand of peer culture. While this may be a benefit, many Muslims find the Muslim community's regulation and surveillance of their behaviors a negative aspect of living Muslim. Several brothers and sisters stated, "Muslims can be so judgmental."

Still, Freitas' omission is a reminder that though Muslim Americans are an important and growing part of American social landscape, they are still excluded from many large-scale studies.

Islamophobia

Lastly, does the current "war on terror" have any effect on Muslim singlehood? It's been acknowledged that the terrorist attacks on the World Trade Centers turned an unwanted and negative spotlight on American Muslims (Turner 2003). Though its effects on singlehood may be indirect, Islamophobia can have a strong influence on the construction of American Muslim identities. Yvonne Haddad, an Islamic scholar explains, "In the last decade and a half, it (*Muslim identity*) has also been profoundly influenced by what Muslims feels is a hostile American environment in which they are being held accountable for the activities of others overseas" (As cited in Al-Johar 2005:557-574).

Media associations of Islam with terrorism push many Muslims to feel America is "Islamaphobic." Post 9-11, "feelings of confidence, faith, and pride in the United States were replaced with fear, apprehension, and uncertainty, especially among the immigrant Muslim population" (Ba Yunus and Kone 2006:172). American Muslims navigate this environment of "moral panic" (Cohen 2002) and are often deemed in the words of Mary Douglas (2002) as "matter out of place" and something to be feared.

No, none of my informants specifically mentioned 9-11 and Islamaphobia as having an effect on their psyches. However, what is important to note is that Islam bashing is a pervasive part of the social world in which young Muslims live and can *subconsciously* affect their religiosity and in turn, their singlehood attitudes and behaviors. At a minimum, it can certainly put a Muslim in a defensive mode where they must play the role of the "Muslim ambassador" to friends, colleagues and even other family members.

In the end, America like any country has both positive and negative aspects. While Muslims are free to practice their religious identities without pressure to convert to Christianity, they also face the challenge of resisting values that contradict their own. The sexual culture and accompanying peer culture push many single Muslims into the third space where Muslim young adults who are have both American and Muslim identities, work to negotiate contradictions.

WOMB # 3
FROM THE DINNER TABLE
FAMILY VALUES & ETHNIC EXPECTATIONS

...
Family are given to you at birth
with your eyes and lips and nose.
They will stick to you wherever you go
and shape how you see
and what you say
and how you are seen
forever.

Excerpt from *What is Family?*
By Anitra L. Freeman from "Families of Poems"

Family values create a child's moral foundation and form the cornerstone of their sense of right and wrong. However, youth make their own decisions and often disagree with their parents' prescriptions. Still, to reduce conflict, many individuals follow tradition in courtship and spousal selection. Here I highlight particular parental values and expectations beginning with religious tenets.

Religiosity

Young people are socialized into parents' religious denominations and frequently adopt their levels of religious commitment. For example, young adults with religious parents often decide not to cohabit without marriage even if they, themselves, do not oppose the practice (Thornton et al 1992). Likewise, young Mormons were shown to hold their parents' views of marriage and singlehood, often feeling positive about their single status if their families support their singlehood, and vice-versa (Darrington et al, 2005).

Parents' also influence the courtship, marriage values and behaviors of their children by influencing the child's own religiosity through either guidance or supervision. For Muslims, the preservation of an Islamic identity is of the utmost importance. One Arab immigrant says:

> I think that the one danger of interaction between my children and non-Muslim children is loss of Muslim identity. I think that integration into the non-Muslim environment has to be done with the sense that we have to preserve our Islamic identity. As long as the activity or whatever the children are doing is not in conflict with Islamic values or ways, it is permissible. But when we see it is going to be something against Islamic values, we try to teach our children that this is not correct to our beliefs and practices. They understand it and they are trying to cope with that (Aswad and Bilge 1996:19).

During singlehood, Muslim parents are often concerned about male-female relationships and many do not allow their children to date (Haddad and Lummis 1987). One Lebanese immigrant father says,

> Dating is not our way of life. The way it is done is ridiculous. I see some people who date one person for three days, then drop them… I am not against finding yourself a partner, but I am against the way they abuse this 'dating.' I don't have as much problem with boys dating girls as I do with girls dating (Haddad and Lummis 1987:139).

Setting gender differences aside for a moment, both quotes above hail from studies focused on the Islamic values held by immigrant Muslims, namely Arab and South Asian (Aswad and Bilge 1996; Haddad and Lummis 1987). However, many of the same values are held by indigenous Muslims, e.g. African-Americans. In *African-American Islam*, McCloud (1995) argues that African-American Muslim parents "pay a great deal of attention to their children's level of sexuality and feel that American society is far too permissive with respect to the sexual relationships of youth" (McCloud 1995:112). If we remember for a moment, that the sexuality of youth and young adults has long been a major concern and often the subject of investigation, for example Mead's Coming of Age in Samoa, we see that Muslim parents are not alone in this regard.

Ethnicity/Race

Muslim families may share a universal religion but they come from a diverse range of ethnic/racial heritages (Carolan et al 2000). A rough estimate of American Muslim demographics is 20% South Asian, 24% Arab, 26% African American, and 24% other (African, White, Latino, Asian, Native American and all –in-between) (Mir 2006). These racial lines of difference often become the bases of Muslim family values. In fact, several informants interpret their parents' actions and views as more cultural, than Islamic, in nature. For example, Mirza, a 24-year old Pakistani-American states,

> Even Pakistanis who aren't outwardly religious will behave in a certain way. For example, I know a lot of people who won't pray 5 times a day but they're totally against something like dating, pre-marital sex, consumption of alcohol. That's how my family was for most of my childhood and much of my adolescence. It's not like my parents were against religion, it was just more apathy and they simply needed something to trigger some sort of change.

Fatima, also Pakistani American, believes these actions are often based on the family's need and desire to maintain their social status. As a result, religiously acceptable activities, like men and women hanging out in a group, or dating with a chaperone, are often prohibited. Fatima says,

> You can go out but with family, but usually that doesn't happen. It's more like you'll get to hang out at each other's houses because no one wants to look bad and send their 23-year-old daughter with a man (or men) she's not even engaged to. Even if they take a chaperone with them (hence it would be *halal* (Islamically permissible!).

Endogamy

Contemporary Muslim young adults also criticize endogamy, the cultural tradition to marry someone of the same background (Grewal 2008). Grewal's analysis of inter-racial Muslim marriage highlights "a generation tug-of-war between 'cultural' (immigrant) parents and 'religious' children" (Grewal 2008:3).

> The first generation grew up in Muslim societies where particular cultural practices (constructions of beauty, marital endogamy, etc.) are naturalized and taken for granted. However, the second generation, raised in the U.S. often dismisses its parents' practices as both racist and "un-Islamic" (Grewal 2008:3).

Young Muslims who choose to be "Muslim first", with religion the most salient aspect of their life, may be more willing to marry outside of their racial/ethnic background (Al-Johar 2005). Grewal raises an interesting point. While the term "cultural" often takes on a negative connotation amongst the younger generation, it is ironic that the younger generation does not "recognize its own American sensibilities as cultural and constructed in the same way as those of their parents" (Grewal 2008:3). In response to one mother who preferred cousin marriages, Grewal notes, "young Muslims raised in the US have also internalized the secular, anti-racist rhetoric that permeates American media and school curricula as well as the cultural norms couched in medical terms that stigmatize practices such as cousin marriages." One Arab informant who acknowledged the influence of America in her views recounts,

> It's so hard to marry [someone] of your same race. We're in America, we go to school with different people our entire lives. And then parents say I don't care if you've been friends with white, black, red, whatever, brown [Muslims]. Those are not people that you can fall in love with (Grewal 2008:17-18).

Ajeenah, a Pakistani informant in this study stated,

> Well a simple explanation (for endogamy) is that they haven't been exposed to other cultures like we have so the

> thought of marrying their daughter in another culture is scary to them. They think they might dissolve me or something.

White Skin. Not surprisingly given the history of colonization and racial stratification within the U.S., spousal selection continually extends beyond religious endogamy, beyond racial endogamy and even beyond ethnic endogamy to phenotypical characteristics – in particular skin color. Grewal (2008) argues that many Arab and South-Asians privilege whiteness and that intra-racism is "a reflection of self-hatred, the internalization of notions of inferiority and defect (and) perhaps the most tragic scar left by systematic racism." Abdullah, a young Syrian states,

> I think [whiteness] is the ultimate beauty standard. "She's so pretty, she's white-skinned." That's always the line [in Franklin and] in Syria… My mother is very white and people are always surprised she's Arab. And she wants me to marry someone who looks like us (Grewal 2008:9).

Grewal argues that passing as white, was and is one way immigrants distance themselves from racial minorities and "climb the economic ladder." In the quest of seemingly economic and social benefits, the spirit of Islam, which promotes cohesion between Muslims "despite any racial or cultural differences," is neglected (Yamani 1998).

We also know from Islamic history, that Prophet Muhammad (pbuh) engaged in and conducted inter-tribal/ ethnic marriages in part to create political and social alliances amongst peoples. It appears too, that that benefit is no longer seen as a major influence on parents' views on acceptable mates.

Naturally, racial endogamy is not particular to Arab and Desi Americans. Black/White interracial relationships have a long history in America. Think of *Guess Who's Coming to Dinner,* a revolutionary 1967 film in which a black man and a white woman attempt to marry. The woman's father speaks volumes about the ways inter-racial marriages were viewed (and are often viewed today):

> As for you two and the problems you're going to have, they seem almost imaginable… I'm sure you know what you are up against. There will be 100 million people right

> here in this country who will be shocked, offended, and appalled at the two of you (line from Guess Who's Coming to Dinner 1967).

Though the Supreme Court legalized interracial marriages that same year, now over 40 years later, U.S. society still has racial borders (Childs 2005). Child's recent investigation on Black/White interracial marriages highlights how prejudice against interracial marriages still exists but is now expressed differently. While interracial marriages were openly defiled during the 40s-60s, there is now a more passive discursive strategy of acknowledgement, without personal engagement, in interracial relationships (Childs 2005). You often hear comments like, *"I don't have a problem with it. But I prefer if my children did not marry outside."*

Blacks often consider racial endogamy an important African-American community norm (Hill Collins in Childs 2005).

> Choosing to date or marry interracially is frowned upon because it is seen as an effect of white domination and internalization by black people of a complex and debilitating prejudice and self-hatred against themselves that makes them perceive whites as superior, and that by associating with whites they can elevate their position (Childs 2005:80).

Others focus more on self-protection from prejudice than self-hatred. For example, one of Childs' focus group respondents stated she wanted her daughter to find a "black husband," because there is no reason for her child "to go over to that other group that doesn't want you anyways." She did not want her daughter "in a situation where she could get hurt." Other members of the focus group agreed that discouraging interracial relationships for loved ones was often not only an acceptable practice, but a necessary one. The White college students of Childs' study felt the same. One student said, "My parents are not prejudiced … they are completely open-minded, but [their concern] comes out of how others would act" (Childs 2005:112).

Naturally, many young adults go along with parental expectations in order to facilitate greater social approval and "easier" marriages (Thornton et al 1992). For example, speaking on interracial marriages, in particular the story of Tariq who was rejected by his fiance's South Asian parents (see chapter 11), Nadia, a Pakistani sister in this study said, *"They (parents) have to show face in their respective communities… [I'm sure] they personally could deal with it (inter-racial marriage) but people who know them is what they probably don't want to deal with."* Nadia is open to an interracial marriage, but for family reasons also plans to marry another Pakistani.

So Who's In and Who's out?

How do families decide who constitutes an "outsider"? Is the decision based on shared values, language, phenotype, geography? What happens when for example, two people from different cultures have more commonalities than differences - perhaps due to a shared level of education and professional social groups (Breger and Hill 1998)? Grewal recounts interracial marriage between Muslims,

> poses a 'boundary dilemma' that forces them to consider the meaning and consequences of 'marrying out' and to 'confront questions about the definition, meaning and significance of the boundaries that mark their identity' (Kibria 1997:524 in Grewal 2008:13).

Thus, who may constitute an outsider today, may not be an outsider tomorrow. I will not attempt to make overarching generalizations, but the discussion goes back to Anderson's idea of an "imagined community." People *feel* like they share common values with others in a particular group based on blood, some shared historical, social or political construct. Often times this may be more geographically based than socially based. I'll just cite one short example from Grewal:

> The young people… think that, well, it's not *haram* [forbidden, sinful] to marry out, so what's the big deal? But the prophet didn't say that. I mean, you have to start in and then go out. Nowadays, girls just say no to suitors without a good reason and that's *haram*. First you have to consider your cousins. If they are not good, then you look at other Indian boys. If you still can't, then Pakistanis. Arabs and other Muslims should be last. But the first thing some of these girls do is look outside even though they have very good cousins. They say nobody marries

> cousins in America but that's our tradition (a South Asian mother in Grewal 2008:16).

This brings me to one final thought on interracial marriages. I have noted that passing and coveting whiteness have been used to climb the economic ladder. Interestingly, it has been documented that the social acceptance of interracial marriages is stronger amongst marriages between peoples of more wealth, adding yet another level of ambiguity in the realm of acceptable spouses (Breger and Hill 1998).

Gender

Within each of the cultural wombs mentioned - Islam, America and family - gender expectations come into play, however families are often the first structure to genderize children. As the Lebanese father quoted prior states, "I don't have as much problem with boys dating as I do with girls dating" (Haddad and Lummis 1987:139). Both males and females spoke of these types of double standards. Irrespective of race/ethnicity, families tended to restrict female social behavior more so than that of males. Take for example, the statement found in an advice column on Muslim Girl magazine, a bimonthly for Muslim teens,

> My parents seem to think that my reputation will be ruined if I sleep over at my best friend's house after her 16th birthday party. The other girls who are sleeping over aren't Muslim, and their parents are fine with it. Why can't my parents trust me, and why do they have such unfair rules for me? They never object if my brother spends a weekend at his friend's house (Excerpt from Muslim Girl Magazine in Garfoli 2007).

Often parents employ these types of restrictions for the protection of "vulnerable" and "weak" females. For example, Nailah, a 28 year old African-American states,

> I remember them (parents) saying boys play rough. Don't play with them. At one point, don't talk to them. In my neighborhood kids used to mess around a lot, like in the laundrymat of the building….. I must've been under ten.

> Kids started around that age, maybe a little younger, you were bound to get felt up if you didn't hold your guard. A little older and there was sex too. It was kinda scary but, I knew they were right. It was restrictive, but I learned from experience that boys really did play rough and once you start playing with them, it's hard to control the situation.

While the males were not protected from physical harm, many young men were raised to protect themselves from emotional harm. They were pushed to guard their feelings, prepare to accept the responsibility of taking care of women and to be *strong* members of the community. Often the biggest impediment to marriage was a lack of finances. This study revealed several assumptions about Muslim male singlehood. For example, many assumed that men primarily marry to fulfill physical needs. However, while that was certainly one factor in the decision to marry, the men of this study also longed for companionship and family life. Experiencing legal sex was not the only reason to end singlehood. In addition, many women assumed singlehood for men is easy, "they don't have to be single if they don't want to be." This study also debunks that myth. Muslim men struggle to end singlehood just as much as Muslim women. It is a community problem, not simply a gender problem.

In conclusion, because of its importance, I explored both "family talk," the ideas expressed by parents, siblings and extended family, as well as family structure (e.g. marital status of parents, number of siblings, etc). Naturally, parental attitudes varied from liberal attitudes towards Islam to strict interpretations of Islamic law. For example, some informants were allowed to have mixed-gender friendships as long as the relationships were "respectful" and non-physical. However, other families did not allow mixed-gender friendships or even conversations.

CHAPTER SUMMARY

In order to contextualize the beliefs and attitudes of single Muslims, this chapter focused on three cultural wombs that contribute to the development of young Muslims: Islam, America and Family/Ethnicity. Basic tenets of Islam were highlighted including a belief in God, the

Prophethood of Muhammad and in an afterlife, which affect the actions of Muslims. Islam also covets marriage as the ideal state of humankind. Moreover, Muslims perform certain daily actions such as prayer, and yearly actions like fasting, which contribute to the construction of an Islamic identity. However, how Muslims "practice" their Islam is in part based on the other two wombs explored, i.e. America and family.

Under America, I focused on individualism, the sex culture, and college life. Individualism, and the view that each individual has the right to take control of his/her life outside of parental or societal expectations, can impact several parts of singlehood including spousal selection and religious choice. Another pervasive aspect of life in America pertains to sex. Though Islam prohibits pre-marital sex, American popular culture portrays extramarital sexual behavior as a normal, perfectly acceptable part of life which can present a moral challenge to Muslims. Finally, Muslims live in a society that equates their faith with terrorism, which could sway some Muslims to "play down" their Muslim identities.

Lastly, families influence not only the religiosity of a young Muslim but also how they relate to their ethnic and national identities. Although American Muslims can all relate to Islam on one level or another, various ethnic identities often trump the prescriptions of an Islamic identity. That is to say, families' expectations and behaviors, like marital endogamy, may be more in line with their ethnic/racial backgrounds than Islamic theology. These distinctions also seep into the gender differences. For example, women's actions were often restricted more than their male relatives. All of this information helps to place the experiences documented in Part II into greater perspective.

REFLECTIONS

Think about the Wombs that Bore you. How have these contributed to your identities? Which parts of the wombs do you accept? Which parts do you reject? Why?

PART II

Eight Reasons American Muslims Struggle With Singlehood

3

Reason # 1
To be or not to be Muslim

Shahadah, the first pillar of faith in Islam, is to declare a belief in one God, and to affirm Muhammad (pbuh) as God's last messenger. When born, children of Muslim parents vicariously live their parents' *shahadah* who groom them to speak like a Muslim, eat like a Muslim, dress like a Muslim, think like a Muslim and behave like a Muslim, at least according to their (parents') definition of "Muslim." However, there comes a time (usually in either high school or college), when young Muslims become aware that parental expectations are often not valued or even considered "normal" in the greater society. When confronted with this reality, they may question Islam and their Muslim practice. As a result, judging the morality of singlehood behavior is difficult because they have not yet decided whether or not to be Muslim, and whether or not to follow Islamic rules.

For example, Nadirah, an African-American college sophomore, was born and raised a Muslim. Her parents are active in the community and along with her three siblings, she grew up attending the *masjid* on a regular basis. However, Nadirah has never studied the religion on her own and though she currently self-identifies as a Muslim, she is not sure she will always be Muslim. Here she explains why she is open to marrying a non-Muslim.

> I haven't really found myself religiously yet so I do want to keep my options open. I already know a marriage with two different religions won't work but I'm not sure if I want to be Muslim. You know everyone is born into a specific religion and I believe you don't have to be that for the rest of your life if you don't want to. I'm just trying to explore my options.

Muslims like Nadirah demand the right to choose their religion for themselves. Being born Muslim does not mean they will remain Muslim. Though this may appear to be a spin off from individualism, the Quran states, "Let there be no compulsion in religion" (Quran 2:256) meaning, no one can force another person to be Muslim. Islam is something a person must decide for themselves.

THE POPULAR GUY

Like Nadirah, Ali was born and raised Muslim but has also explored his options and made his own decisions about what is right and wrong. As a Californian teen, Ali desired to be "just a regular teenager" and accordingly began to build a life outside of the *masjid.* He stayed busy with several extra-curricular activities like debate and sports and also had several girls with whom he "fooled around." Even with them, Ali postponed having sex.

> I did not want to even think about having sex. My dad told me that I if I got a girl pregnant that I would not be able to go away to college, and I would have to get a job and support the girl and the baby. That scared the crap out of me… I like kissing, and "fooling" around but I was not interested in sex. I had been helping to raise my younger siblings so I understood what babies meant. I had a few intense crushes, one White, one Jewish and one Black.

Ali admits his behaviors may have fallen outside of his parents' and community's expectations but he never played the "guilt game." He says, *"I knew it was not what was traditionally acceptable so I kept it in my own realm and did not blast it to the world. Most people saw me as a happy guy who did not date."* While living at home, Ali wanted to be a good student and respect his parents' rules. It was not until he left home for college that he used the freedom to experiment with different lifestyles. He began to read about other spiritual paths such as Buddhism and Hinduism. And his new social scene included parties, alcohol, marijuana and other drugs.

"Curiosity" about life outside of Islam is what pushes many Muslims to experiment in college

Though Ali's lifestyle changed dramatically, he always identified as Muslim. He still attended *jumah* (Friday prayer service), observed many of the regular prayers and during *Ramadan*, the Muslim month of fasting, he would "clean up real good." He lived in what Bhabha described as the liminal, middle ground *third space* between Islamic ideals, popular American singlehood and his own personal desires.

As for relationships, during college and beyond, Ali describes himself as a "smoking hippie" who was into "secular" women. He began a slew of intimate relationships, none of which culminated in marriage. When one girlfriend revealed she did not want to raise her children as Muslims, Ali realized their lifestyles were incompatible. Disappointed and heartbroken, he began to reevaluate his life.

> I moved to a new city and finally decided to stop drinking. To finally start growing up and get my Islamic studies on. I went to study Arabic at [an American Islamic Institution] and was for the first time in my life around a cool group of Muslim peers. Allahu Akbar! (God is Greater!) … I thought, I have come a long way away from where I was in my parent's house. How do I get back there? But I was not hard on myself. I made gradual changes so that I could internalize them.

Ali's changes included increasing prayer and studying the Quran more. He discovered that what he truly desired was a family and that the other activities simply provided him with an excuse to postpone marriage. Upon reflection he states,

> [Alcohol was] fun. I only drank when I had finished my work and I was a lightweight. I like to smoke weed more than that but I had a blast in college experimenting with different drugs. *I guess it was a big smokescreen that veiled me from my real purpose and responsibility [which was] figuring out how to make money and be a man so that I could hold down some woman financially and also be her spiritual anchor! (emphasis mine)*

Now that Ali's spirituality and connection to Allah was getting stronger, he slowly began to long for marriage and fatherhood. But finding a wife, a Muslim wife was now the issue. Ali felt like he did not know any Muslim women who *"seemed like they understood the nuances of life a bit."* So initially he continued to have relationships with more "secular" women. He also viewed many of the Muslim women he knew as "rigid" in their behavior and unwilling to accept someone with his background and worldview.

> Sadly it seems I am not MAN enough. Many men feel that way, that they are not worthy. Its a lack of confidence, I have struggled with that and still do. Lately I have been more aware of it and am addressing that.

In addition to his personal insecurities, Ali felt like an outsider in the Muslim community. His father was well known in the community but he was not. Ali says, the community did not *"really accept me in the way black people can approve or disapprove each other"* until the Imam began to pull him aside. Feeling rejected, Ali again reverted to what was comfortable - his relationship with Leila, a Palestinian-American whom he had been dating off and on for over four years. Though they tried to make it work, by the time we had our follow up interview, Ali and Leila had ended their relationship for good. Leila was perfect in every way except she was "more secular" than Ali thought. He suspects she covered it up to appease him.

> I have to find a woman that wants to be with the whole me, not just the *dunya* (worldly life) part. At the end of the day, she said we just argued too much and I just got mad that I "wasted" my time trying to be with someone that did not see the value of placing Allah at the center of a relationship. I'm not interested in marrying a non-Muslim.

> I want someone who can balance this life and the next life. Brains so that my children (*inshaAllah*) will have a fuller understanding, not just some rote belief or blind faith.

Given Ali's own gradual personal transformation, his stance on Leila was surprising. Perhaps Leila could also receive a "religious awakening." But Ali is now at the point where he knows exactly what he desires in a wife and he is unwilling to compromise on those key characteristics.

At the present moment, Ali is truly single. He does not have a girlfriend and is working on his relationship with himself and God. Now that Ali is more dedicated to living his life within the boundaries of Islamic behavior, singlehood has become even harder.

> I wish I was not [single] and that I had a *halal* outlet for my physical desires. But I have been blinded by secular society. I've been really going internal to cull out the ways that I have played a victim and thereby being unclear and not confident and *it was all based on my relationship with Allah.* So I am strengthening that so that I can be an anchor to a woman. [I mean] singlehood is boring. (*emphasis mine*)

Ali shows how religiosity (not in the sense of performing rituals, but as an inner connection to God) is a strong predictor of singlehood behavior. During college, Ali's Muslim identity had not yet permeated every aspect of his life, which led him to experiment with other lifestyles. For those who may have observed him, it may have appeared that he had simply given up on Islam, but Ali sees his spiritual development as something he had to grow through to get to where he is today. Islam was always in his heart. And now that his connection to God is stronger, Ali is fully able to concentrate on creating a family.

Ali's challenge now is to fulfill his responsibilities as the financial base of a family. As we shall see later in the text, Ali is ready for marriage and is looking for a wife, but is having trouble finding the right type of *Muslima,* one who is willing to accept his shortcomings. And one who likes to have fun like Ali.

LIVING A DUAL LIFE

I met Tahira when she was in Kalamazoo on business. While giving her a tour of the city, I explained my research and she graciously offered to share her experiences. Like Ali, her story is a vivid example of a young Muslim struggling with conflicting desires: to have fun and be a "normal" student, to be a "good" Muslim, and to find solace in achieving both. For a number of years, Tahira lived a dual life - one that she showed to only a few individuals. While managing two lifestyles was stressful, now that she has come into her own, there exists a new struggle: to find a Muslim husband whom she loves.

Tahira was born and raised in a tight knit Muslim community. Her family lived around the corner from the *masjid* and she attended the neighborhood Muslim school. With boys, Tahira remembers hanging out with male classmates until she received her menarche, *"My parents definitely weren't down with me just chilling with boys past puberty…or really before if there wasn't a reason… so no male friends."* Later, Tahira moved to another Muslim school where post pubertal interactions as well as public boyfriend/girlfriend 'situations', were more commonplace. Tahira, too, desired to have a boyfriend; she just never found the courage.

> I guess it was a combination of things. I thought it was wrong inherently, plus I have always been logical to a fault and I couldn't figure out a way that my parents wouldn't find out [laughing]. I was scared of them finding out, I think more so of their disappointment than their initial reaction. That fear kept me out of a lot of possible trouble during that time.

Tahira's connection to Islam was strengthened during a 17-month hiatus in the Middle East, where her father's job took the family. There, she decided to get more serious about her *deen* (Islamic way of life). She says,

> I think I became Muslim, meaning really deciding that I wanted to be Muslim, while living in the Middle East, so that was high school for me. At the time I was practicing

> more so than I ever had on my own, but the reality of it was that it was so easy to practice when you're secluded.

Upon her return to the U.S., Tahira entered her senior year of high school, this time at a public school where for the first time in life, she found herself as a religious minority.

> It was complete culture shock. I hadn't interacted with the opposite sex in any way in years, or had normal interactions (American normal) with peers. So I think the last year of high school and my first year of college was a huge transition where I was trying to get back to 'normal' – whatever that was. The same temptations that I had prior to leaving crept back into my life, except this time the fear of my parents wasn't as much of a deterrent. I got into things with full knowledge of wrong and I kept away from other things because I felt that was going too far. I always prayed that Allah (SWT – Glory be to God) allowed me to live through the phase because I had the consciousness to know I was in the wrong and I needed to get right. So I would say I knew that I wanted to be Muslim, but I wasn't willing to accept everything that I felt Muslim to be while in college. I allowed myself to explore, with the plan to get right at graduation.

Not many know Tahira's other side. She usually concealed her other life in order to minimize the judgment and negative feedback of other Muslims. Seeming embarrassed, Tahira asks if I am surprised by her disclosures. When I explained that in fact her story was very similar to my own she seemed to relax a bit. In college, away from her parents' rules, 'natural instincts and societal norms' pushed Tahira into the liminal *third space* between her Islamic upbringing and her college environment. She began to date and visit the clubs.

> There were things that I wanted to experience even though it may have been against what I felt a 'good' Muslim was - like going out, less modest clothing, relationships, etc. Basically I kinda gave myself a break from practicing the way I felt I should be in order to

> experience the 'life' that I had always been curious about, but I knew I was putting my soul in danger. And I had every intention to get back straight after the break, which I set to be my graduation from undergrad. For example, just to give you insight on my screwed up mentality (laughing), my most serious relationship in college was very tumultuous because from jump (the beginning). I told the guy that I only planned to marry a Muslim. Now we weren't thinking about marriage or anything but it really bothered him….and why shouldn't it! It's just flat out telling someone 'this is for now, it can go nowhere, enjoy it while it last.'

Though she is embarrassed to think about it now, Tahira feels these experiences were a necessary but hidden part of her development. She lived a double consciousness (Dubois 1903), "*I really perfected my duality in college, I had my Muslim life and hung out with Muslim circles, then the other life…most privy to the other side were my non-Muslim acquaintances in college, I never really mixed the two circles or identities.*" Living a dual life became difficult to manage and created feelings of despair. Tahira gave one example.

It was like I was living two lives, a Muslim life and a "normal" college student life.

> One break while I was in college, I was hanging out with one of my childhood Muslim friends back home. She was one who got married after high school as a virgin, was now in college and considering having a kid. She was very much on the good girl path at that time. Her and her friends were talking about so and so who goes to the club, 'what is she thinking, etc.' All I did was feel so guilty and stay silent because I knew I was going to do that as soon as I got back to school. Honestly, it is not until very recently that I have actively started to break that duality. I think it's an epidemic with our generation, where we are more comfortable around John our co-worker, classmate, friend than we are with Muhammad. And vice versa. So I have

> said screw that recently and decided I needed to be the same around both.

The epidemic Tahira mentions, where Muslims are closer to non-Muslims than other Muslims is a point I discuss more fully later but it is important to note how Tahira's level of anxiety was significantly lower around her non-Muslim friends who did not operate within the same Islamic framework. With them, a tight shirt or flirtatious talk with a man would not be cause for judgment like it would with other Muslims. In fact, several informants recounted keeping secrets from other Muslims because they did not want to be seen as a "bad Muslim."

Tahira felt like she was slipping away from Islam, and needed something to keep her strong. She tried to join the Muslim Student's Association, but the group of mostly South Asian and Arab men made her feel like she wasn't a real Muslim. Rebuffed, she gave up on being with them and in turn found her *hijab* (hair scarf) effective in maintaining a connection to Islam. Covering her hair became the main thing she refused to let go of, *"I felt on some level that if I let that go, I would never come back. So I was one of those scandalous hijabis. I tried to rock my scarf in a less Muslim way when I was being really scandalous [laughing]."* Laughing I interjected, "the bun in the back?" Tahira, "*You know it! (laughing), black scarf, baby hairs out…bunned (laughing).*"

An outward expression of dress, and *hijab* in particular, is one of the most visible differences between single Muslim women and men. Muslim women are seen to portray an inner level of Islam (as I discuss later, *hijab* is often a requirement for many Muslim men), through the cloth they use to adorn their bodies. For Tahira, the bun style (picture a ponytail with the fabric wrapped around at the base of the neck) effectively blurred the lines between her definition of a completely "Muslim" identity, (i.e. not showing the neck and ears), and a regular college student identity, (i.e. no scarf at all). However outward expressions are not always in congruence with what one feels is their "core" identity.

> The way I was brought up, you weren't Muslim if you didn't cover, like you were ignorant if you didn't or something. But when I really looked into it, *(I went through my deprogramming phase in recent years, actually I am still in it in some ways)*, I realized that the Arabic language in the Quran doesn't say you have to cover, it infers *hijab*. The *hadith*

> that is always mentioned is weak and that the requirement of *hijab* comes from scholarship, so with that, that leaves room for other interpretations. Personally, I haven't seen the full evidence making it required, but I am sure the scholarship has researched it more than I have dedicated my time to it, so my personal decision is to stick with it. It's my visible Muslim identity, and I feel it is ridiculous for me to make myself comfortable without it. So I stick with it but I understand that knowledgeable Muslims can take another route because there is room.

Having learned Islam from her parents, Islamic school and her time in the Middle East, Tahira had internalized a brand of Islam that until recently went unquestioned. She is now studying on her own in order to deepen her personal relationship with Islam.

To marry or not to marry

During college and for five years after, Tahira resisted pressure from family and friends to get married. She would use every excuse from their age, to even their shoes to reject someone. But a change of heart was slow coming.

> You have to realize, I tried to turn this magic stick where I had relationships and people I had genuine feelings for, but had reconciled that these weren't long term because of the non-Muslim thing. Then after graduation, I tried to be all *muslimy*, cut all these people out of my life, and just look at people for the purpose of marriage from the get go. Yea that wasn't realistic. That wasn't the way I was used to getting to know people. And plus I had unresolved feelings from old situations. I just had to grow as a independent person and really live life on my own to understand and want to share my life with someone.

Tahira began to let her guard down - she even tried her hand at talking to a Muslim man (for the purpose of marriage), someone she had a crush on growing up. The new process was awkward, she says, *"neither of us had ever really talked to Muslims before so we didn't know what the script was."* Little things that would have seemed so natural before, like hugging, required more forethought. Is this appropriate?

The relationship did not succeed but Tahira learned a lot about herself and her mate preferences. She is now playing the waiting game. She is single by fate, not by choice. This time the difference is that she is more serious about adhering to what she believes is right. She wants to find a husband, not a boyfriend. When the singleness gets too much she leans on her friends:

> When I am really ready to go crazy, I tell a friend and they talk me out of it (laughing) and sometimes, Allah (SWT) just stands in my way, because every now and then I get determined to act out (laughing), but *MashaAllah* (Allah has willed), I have maintained for some time. But *inshaAllah* (if Allah wills) the single thing will be remedied sooner rather than later (laughing).

In the mean time, Tahira is taking advantage of her singlehood and personal time by advancing her career and travelling internationally. While she travels extensively for work, it is not something she anticipates continuing once married. She is now comfortable in her skin, which for her meant relinquishing some "questionable" activities like clubbing. Throughout the text, we shall see some of the other challenges Tahira now faces in her singlehood. She hopes that she is able to help her children to have a strong personal connection to Allah on their own – which may make them less "curious" about life outside of Islam.

REFLECTIONS

How do you identify spiritually/ religiously? When, why and how did you make that decision?

4

Reason # 2
I'VE GOT NEEDS
(PHYSICAL AND EMOTIONAL)

LONELINESS

"Something odd happens when people notice someone who is (or who may be) single or when they think about an adult who may be alone, even temporarily. Their mind seems to leap immediately to notions of loneliness" (DePaulo 2006:55). DePaulo positions this assumption as a stereotype, but I found that indeed, most Muslim young adults who are involuntarily single are lonely. Specifically, they long for the type of feelings that accompany a meaningful romantic relationship. While the word lonely has a lot of negative attachments, it is simply a natural human state and nothing to be ashamed of. Shoot, I've been lonely plenty of times! Here, Nailah, a 28 year-old African American children's artist mentions her experience with loneliness:

> I remember the first time I felt really lonely. I was in Europe in 2003 and I was like, I want someone to share this with. I mean my life is good a lot of the time but I would like to share it with someone. I mean singlehood is Whaaaaaack! I need some luvin!

The situation is similar for Aminah, a former print journalist and current resident of Los Angeles. Her previous lifestyle in the arts was exciting, but she thinks it pales in comparison to what getting married and having children will provide her. She says,

> Although I've traveled all over the world, I didn't feel like I lived. I wanted to do something significant, like get married and have a child. Every time I traveled, it was by myself. I was so lonely and I didn't feel like my job was making me grow, I still felt like I was 18 but I was 28. I should feel different, like sophisticated, and mature… I love Islam. Although I've been extremely lonely, I've been protected from many, many things, and that is due to Islam. Just imagine me in the entertainment industry and not having my Islamic values to protect me...who knows where I would be.

Aminah views Islam's prohibition on intimate relationships outside of marriage as having contributed to her loneliness, but also as a protection from unwanted dangers like HIV and drug abuse. Currently, Aminah is involved with a non-Muslim man whom she may consider marrying. She feels torn between waiting for a Muslim man and marriage, and fulfilling her current emotional needs. She sighs, *"I do (like his companionship) and I didn't have companionship in a LONG time. I thought I was going to die from loneliness."*

Singlehood is whack! I need some lovin! - Nailah

For Jaleela, an African-American teacher, the situation is a bit different. Having married during her junior year of college, shortly after converting to Islam, most of her life as a Muslim was spent married. When she discovered the man she met online, and later came to love, had several secrets including another wife and child, Jaleela was devastated. Her Senegalese husband explained that he was planning to divorce his wife, but as time went by it became apparent he did not intend to divorce his wife back home. He was waiting for Jaleela to accept his other wife, something that she was not willing to do. The final deal breaker came when her husband began to hang out late at night and see other women. Though she loved him, Jaleela found the courage to leave. Now two years after their six-year marriage ended, she finds the transition to living as a single Muslim again very trying. She says,

> Singlehood? It's ok, but I'd rather be married (laughing). It's difficult to be around couples because it makes me miss being married. And it's hard to go to events and things alone. Sometimes it's hard to come home from work and be alone and eat dinner alone especially during Ramadan.

What Nailah, Aminah and Jaleela describe are not "women's issues." Yet whenever I broached the subject of loneliness, people often assumed it was women who expressed loneliness more so than men. In reality, several brothers expressed emotional desires, albeit without using the word "lonely." When I asked one African-American brother "*Do you ever get lonely?*" he responded, "*Yeah, we all do. Everyone has needs; it's not only about sex with us guys.*" The issue seemed to be more with word usage than meaning.

One of the reasons men in this study may not have used the word "lonely" is that it is not socially acceptable for men to desire a real emotional attachment or to display their emotions at all. Petrie writes, "One of the roles men play is that of the rational being devoid of strong emotions. Profound feelings, it is thought, will interfere with the male task, whether that means making it at the nine-to-five or making it at war" (Petrie 1982). In our society, tenderness and expressions of companionship are often seen as signs of weakness. Accordingly, the men in this study often used other phrases to describe their feelings. I was much more likely to hear statements like, "*Yes, I'm really ready to get married and start a family*" more than "*I'm lonely.*" As a woman, I have not experienced life from a man's perspective and have therefore asked my husband to author "A Letter to the Brothers." I would encourage all men to read that section of the appendices.

Social Scene. Creating an active social life can loosen the focus on marriage and help Muslim young adults cope with loneliness. Some like Fatima, a Pakistani-American student, throw themselves into school, work or other busy activities to keep their minds off of their single status. In an online chat she explained, "*that's why I love being a grad student. You get so busy you can forget …(plus) a lot of us try to make ourselves feel better by having a large circle of friends so that at least we have somebody* ☺." Yet even with tons of great friends, Fatima admits she still gets those "lonely moments."

From the outside, Muslim singles can appear to have it all - great jobs, clothes, friends...but often deep down there lies a longing for something more. Many are willing to wait for marriage but they still feel robbed of the love, intimate touch and joy that a meaningful relationship can bring. On top of this, there is a stigma on the word "lonely" as if it is some type of deviant human emotion. Muslim singles struggle to be comfortable both within their singlehood as well as expressing their desire to end it and the accompanying loneliness.

DATING

> Dear Bilqis, I am a 17-year-old *Muslima.* I always try to follow the religion of Islam. It is the month of Ramadan right now, and lately I just feel like I really really want to get married. I feel like I'm getting tortured or something because I am not married yet. I do know I am young, but there have been times where I have had dreams or visions where they kind of gave me good tidings. Those cheer me up a bit, but I don't know what to do. I definitely don't want a boyfriend or any *haram* relationship but I'm so confused I don't know what to do. Can you help me? *(Reprinted from a marriage post on www.zawaj.com)*

Do Muslims have girlfriends or boyfriends? When I asked this question I was often told, "Premarital sex is not allowed in Islam," or "boys and girls are not allowed to be alone together without a chaperone." Which meant "No." However, when probed, almost every participant in this study spoke of examples or experiences that contradict that ideal. For example, during one conversation with Lisa, a 22-year old White convert, it was not until I asked specific questions regarding her activities with her fiancé that she moved from stating *"it is wrong to be alone with a male"* to describing a typical outing with her recent fiancé going to the movies unaccompanied. When asked if her behavior could be categorized as dating, she hesitated and said *"Well, I don't really have any choice, my family is not Muslim and his family is not here in the country."*

I can understand Lisa's hesitation with revealing her courtship activities. She may have been afraid that I may judge her. Other than to God, there is no confession in Islam and it is very difficult for Muslims to admit to a researcher that they have "sinned" or done something that may be viewed as un-Islamic. Many are worried they will be labeled a "bad" Muslim. The Muslim community is generally understanding of "un-Islamic" actions *before* being Muslim. However, once accepting Islam, all of that behavior is to cease. Muslims are no longer afforded the ability to speak, without reservation, about experiences that go against common understandings of proper Islamic behavior. Post-conversion and post-declaration (for born Muslims) temptation is to be met and defeated with strong faith.

Nevertheless, Muslims do indeed date. So why the taboo? An often quoted *hadith* of the Prophet Muhammad states that whenever a man and a woman are alone together, *Shaitan* (Satan) is the third person. Embedded in the gender separation that many Muslims practice is the attitude or belief that humans are highly physical beings and that our physical needs can overtake our ethos or our psychological understandings. In other words, sex is a powerful force in human action. Elijah, a 30-something African-American states,

> It's (a friendship with the opposite sex) is obviously looked down upon due to the risk of potential mistakes. Even if people do not intend to develop feelings for one another, they can after a time and it can lead to people committing actions that they should not commit. Aside from obvious sins like adultery or fornication, it can also introduce doubts and the habits of sinning, which can have further ramifications for people.

The following question posted on a public website highlights a similar view. Though the question is from a teenager, the dilemma raised could easily affect one of my informants. The response, given by what appears to be a somewhat traditional conservative Muslim, is the type of advice Muslims often receive in response to their desires.

> *Question:* I am 15 years old. I feel that I am a fairly religious person and try to pray five times a day. I respect and honor you and your teachings of Islam. That is why I need

your advice. I must admit that I kind of have a girlfriend at school that I like very much. She is oriental. I know I shouldn't have a girlfriend but it just happened, I didn't plan on it. She is 16 and neither did she. She has led a very bad life with several foster parents and physical and sexual advances. She cares for me very much and will almost do anything I say. My original goal was to make her Muslim but then I started liking her. No the *Shaitan* had nothing to do with this because I have prayed very long and hard for this to happen. My question is whether or not I should ask her to change her religion. I don't want her to do it because of me because she would not have real faith in her heart. I wish to leave my name anonymous. Please help.

Answer I am pleased to know that you consider yourself a religious person and pray five times a day. It means that you want to obey Allah and His Prophet Muhammad - peace be upon him. If that is the case then you should not have a girlfriend. It is not allowed for a Muslim boy to have girlfriend or for a Muslim girl to have a boyfriend. Howsoever pure your intentions may be, the danger is that it will lead you to sin. Or at least you will be alone with each other and spend more time together. The Prophet - peace be upon him- said that whenever a man and a woman who are not related to each other as Mahram meet alone, the Shaitan comes as a third person in their midst. You should be friendly with your classmates, boys and girls both; but do not take a girl as your intimate friend. Of course, homosexuality is also forbidden in Islam. So do not take a boy either as your intimate friend in the "gay sense" of the word.

If your friend, not girlfriend, is interested in Islam, by all means help her to become Muslim. Give her the Islamic books and ask her to attend Islamic meetings and lectures. Let her accept Islam by her own will. Do not force her or put any pressure on her to become Muslim. You are still very young. I suggest that you give more time to your studies now. Do not worry too much to go out of your

> ways to show sympathies to other females. May Allah bless you and keep you on the right path.

The example above illustrates the ambivalence of Muslim youth and young adults concerning romantic feelings. The common response from the adult community is much like that above. Most often, the feelings of the young person are simply pushed aside and the individual is expected to "focus on school." Because their feelings are not validated, many choose to simply live their lives in private like Ali and Tahira, or may choose to leave Islam fully. The young man's emotional needs were not addressed in the answer.

Solutions

Like Lisa, many Muslims are looking for solutions to the issue of male/female relationships. Asma Gull Hasan (2000) recounts an online discussion in which a man "seemed to suggest that American Muslims needed to come up with solutions to the problem of what young Muslims should do who are not being allowed to date because of Islamic traditions, yet are not marrying at a young age. Was there any room for dating in American Islam (Hasan 2000:125)?" When I posed this question to Jason, 26, he responded:

> I think everything is really about intentions. So you can shake hands, hug, do all types of stuff. Anything that has a non-suggestive connotation to society, meaning suggesting a sexual interest. I do think dating is helpful for some people. Too many times we set our selves up for failure in the society because we try to adopt exotic or non-indigenous gender interaction norms. But then at the same time we want to get married and our chief complaint is '*I want to get to know the person but what do I do?*' so that always poses the question, '*How do you get to know somebody without doing the "haram"?*' And so is our plight. I think if two families say that '*Ok, yall can see each other but just know down the line yall better have something going on*', I think its fine. I mean people do it anyway, like talking on the internet. So

> this way you could involve the family. Talk to your mom about her and stuff like that.

For Jason's suggestions to take root, the stigma on male/female relationships would first have to be removed. His discussion also leads me to a point of clarification. Though most Muslims agree that dating in the sense of a woman and man going out alone is prohibited, the rules do vary with dating in the sense of getting to know someone for the purpose of marriage. In fact, there has recently been an explosion of the usage of the term "intended" to signify two people are planning to marry. They may or may not be formally engaged but their intentions are to see if they are compatible for marriage. Depending on the family, dating rules are sometimes relaxed during this "intended" stage. Still overall, the predominate view is that dating should be either prohibited or limited because it can lead to sex, a belief substantiated by several studies (e.g. Thornton 1995).

> ***They keep saying "fast" if you want sex, but that doesn't always work for me...***

The Niyah Filter

Jason's thoughts also bring up something I call *The Niyah (nee-ya) filter.* Niyah is an Arabic word that is used to mean a person's intentions. In hybridizing Islamic teachings and American culture, many young Muslims look to the intent behind an action to determine its appropriateness. This is in part based on the following *hadith*:

> Actions are (judged) by motives *(niyah)*, so each man will have what he intended. Thus, he whose migration *(hijrah)* was to Allah and His Messenger, his migration is to Allah and His Messenger; but he whose migration was for some worldly thing he might gain, or for a wife he might marry, his migration is to that for which he migrated. (Prophet Muhammad, Al-Bukhari & Muslim)

With this, activities like clubbing, can be deemed appropriate as Nadirah, the young lady who has not decided if she will be Muslim or not stated in a recent story:

> Now I just gotta throw this into the atmosphere. I went to the club Friday right and my parents do not understand why I go. Now all my friends are real lady like, we just go to dress up and have fun. We are not the type to dance all nasty and stuff because nowadays dancing is a very close to sex, very very close. But my dad says its unIslamic to go to stuff like that and it makes no sense to me because for the most part everyone just stands around and talk some times…maybe dance with their friends - I was dancing with my friends.

Symbolic interactionism, a theory put forth by Herbert Blumer to explain the meanings of actions, suggests:

1) Humans relate to objects and living beings based on the meanings we have for such objects and beings;
2) Our meanings for objects and beings are derived from communication and relationships – that is, from social interactions with others; and
3) These meanings move between the social to the individual and are therefore shaped and guided by an interpretive process undertaken by an individual subject (Blumer 1969:50 in Madison 2006:64).

A *niyah filter*, i.e. checking in on the intentions of actions and the meanings of those actions, can shift in relation to the constructs of the time. Throughout this study, I found several instances of *niyah filtering*, especially when it pertains to activities with the opposite sex, dating, hanging out, etc.

SEX AND THE SINGLE MUSLIM

Single Muslims do not live in a protected, asexualized bubble. As Holland and Eisenhart (1990) argue, even college campuses support the sex culture, something I recently realized when I noticed a condom vending machine in the computer lab. To me, the message conveyed to students is "sex is always just around the corner." While some argue that condom machines promote safe sex and reduce unwanted pregnancies, abstinence does also. However, signs promoting abstinence on college campuses are often absent - perhaps because sex, not abstinence sells in our economy.

So, how are Muslim young adults negotiating these types of environments? Are they having sex in large numbers? Most informants were comfortable expressing a desire for physical intimacy – an obvious benefit of Muslim marriage. And though I did not ask, about 30% of my informants mentioned whether or not they were virgins. Of them, roughly half were virgins and half were not. Nailah, who is saving herself for God and marriage, believes prolonged virginity is unnatural.

> I have hormones. It's serious. I feel like my body is like, we need to make a baby soon. Or at least see the possibility. But it's not only about having kids because I don't want to have kids immediately. But, I do feel a way about it when I am with my friends and relatives who have little children and husbands. It's like - that's really nice [...] Virginity is not supposed to last for decades. And then the people who are out having sex, probably don't feel rushed (to get married) because what does marriage have to offer that would make them rush? I think we are denying ourselves of our own humanity.

During college Nailah was able to resist the urge to engage in sex, partly by limiting relationships. As she grew older her physical desires coupled with emotional desires and loneliness became a source of pain. She believes many of her friends feel the same. When I asked if she thought many brothers were in her position, she replied, "*Hmm, it's hard out there for the brothers.*" Many women informants assumed that Muslim brothers experiment with sex prior to marriage at a much higher rate than the sisters.

However, contrary to popular belief, virgin Muslim men do exist. True, resisting the sex culture is a struggle, but some Muslim men would never think of stepping outside of the boundaries of Islam. For example, Adel is a 23-year-old recently married African-American man. Prior to getting married, he never had a girlfriend. Here he explains why,

> I think it was party because of my upbringing. I mean I really just believe it is wrong. But I also just didn't have the

> opportunity. I never dated nor had a girlfriend. I mean if the opportunity is available, nine times out of ten someone is gonna take it.

Adel's male cousin is also a virgin. Though dating may indeed offer the opportunity to have sex, it appears that for most people, the decision to have or not to have sex is more connected to the level of integration in Islam. The more someone identifies with a Muslim identity, the less likely they are to engage in pre-marital sexual behavior. Sure, the temptation may arise, but many feel the love of their Muslim identity and Islam trumps that desire. For others, the definition of fornication is limited to intercourse only. So what does "sex" really mean?

Promiscuous Virgins

In many cultures around the world, virginity is a requirement for marriage. Of course, the burden of proof has always been placed on women. For example, in India, Pakistan and parts of Africa, a new bride may bring out a bloodied sheet to prove her virginity. Naturally, many immigrant American Muslims hold the same cultural values here in the United States and have passed them on to their children. A few sisters mentioned that while growing up, they were sometimes afraid of breaking their hymens and as a result, they limited activities like riding bikes and other sports. During my research, I also discovered a shocking trend: some European Muslim women have sexual intercourse and then have a surgery to repair their hymens prior to their wedding date. A newspaper article quoted a cosmetic surgeon who performs the surgery, "If you're a Muslim woman growing up in more open societies in Europe, you can easily end up having sex before marriage. So if you're looking to marry a Muslim and don't want to have problems, you'll try to recapture your virginity" (Sciolino and Mekhennet 2008). Clearly, in this case, the reasoning behind the repair is for more social and cultural reasons rather than religious reasons. To me, the doctor's statement suggests that individuals have no will power at all and that they are easily taken over by society.

While a discussion about hymens was not a major theme of this study, a discussion of what it means to be a virgin did arise. For some informants, virginity applies to sexual intercourse only and does not include outercourse or other sexual activities. One informant indicated that she has "received a few favors in her day," (namely oral sex) but she has never *had* sex (intercourse). Often people interacted with the sexual peer culture by engaging in sexual activities, but stopping shy of actual intercourse. In a sense preserving their virginity.

Pornography. To abstain from sexual intercourse, some Muslim young men turn to pornography and masturbation to release their sexual tensions, a sensitive subject that I did not attempt to investigate. However, Talib, a college junior, did in fact discuss his struggle with a pornography addiction (something he believes is quite common among other men). He tried to stop over the years, and has recently begun to reduce his time on the internet. My curiosity peaked, I conducted a brief investigation into pornography addictions and Muslims. I discovered that SoundVision, a popular website among American Muslims, publishes both a "12-step Guide to Fight Pornography Addiction" as well as "29 Tips for Teens Struggling with an Addiction to Pornography." Some of the tips include:

> Tip #2: Surf the web or watch TV. when others are around
> Tip #3: Remember Allah is watching you
> Tip #4: If it happens, seek forgiveness & don't insist on doing it
> Tip #5: Just get up and leave
> Tip #9: Avoid those involved in pornography
> Tip #10: Avoid things that lead to sin
> Tip #11: Develop a more productive schedule
> Tip #17: Look for alternative entertainment

It appears that a pornography addition is a major struggle for quite a few people. Some men and women also use masturbation in order to resist having "real" sex, a practice deemed unacceptable in Islam. Like other secret habits, these behaviors often become a source of shame and guilt. To protect their reputations, they tend to deal with the issues on their own, or outside of the Muslim community.

Suppressing the Desire

After "get married," the most common advice given to Muslim young adults regarding the desire for physical intimacy is to follow the *hadith*, "Young men, those of you who can support a wife should marry, for it keeps you from looking at women and preserves your chastity; but those who cannot should fast, for it is a means of cooling passion" (Prophet Muhammad in Bukhari). Of course, this fast would also involve an increase in prayer and spiritual reflection. However, many find this solution to lack effectiveness. One male informant stated, *"All they say is fast, fast, fast. Man I would be fasting every dang ole day! How is that gonna work?"* Another said, *"Fasting? Yeah, but that doesn't really work in my opinion, that hunger doesn't die easily."*

When I raised the topic of pre-marital sex and natural desires during an impromptu discussion at a *masjid* I visited, Brother Muhammad, a Tunisian immigrant in his 60's related a story that goes along with "Tip #19: Remember your mom and sister" from SoundVision's list:

> A youth approached the Prophet and asked him to permit him to commit *zina* (fornication). The companions of the Prophet were outraged and rebuked him, but the Prophet (pbuh) asked him to draw closer and sit before him. He asked, " *Would you accept this from your mother?*" to which the man replied *"Certainly not, who could accept this from his mother?"* The Prophet went on to ask him, " *Would you accept this from your daughter, your sister, or your aunt?*" to which the man repeated the same answer " *Certainly not, who could accept this?*" So the Prophet put his hand on his chest and said " *Oh God, forgive his sins, purify his heart, and safeguard his chastity.*" The youth left so repulsed that the desire left him.

Brother Muhammad followed the story with his own advice, *"We have to tell them it's wrong. It is wrong and a grave sin. Abstinence is the key."* Although everyone in the group agreed with Brother Muhammad, they were looking for real world solutions. Naim, an African American convert age 28 added, *"Everybody knows that it's wrong, that's not the question. The question is what are we going to do in response? People need real life solutions, not just holy words.*

Another informant, Elijah, a professor in his mid-30s suggested,

> The best way is to obviously GET MARRIED! But if they cannot, then aside from fasting there are many mental and physical disciplines one can adopt to combat the urges and desires when one is single. Serious intellectual or academic endeavors combined with a strong study/practice of spirituality can be quite formidable. Exercise and physical rigor are also great ways to alleviate the stress of strong carnal desires.

When Muslims give the advice "get married", they take for granted that getting married is not a 1-day process. In fact, this entire study is based on the difficulties in ending unwanted singlehood. Not only must individuals find a spouse, they must find the right spouse. Plus they must deal with all of the pressure that comes along with the process.

REFLECTIONS

For Singles: How do you handle loneliness? If you have them, what has been useful to quell the physical desires? Is it an issue?

For others: What advice do you give to single individuals who desire sex and want to be married but are not yet married?

5

Reason # 3: The Pressure is Overwhelming!

While carpooling to a Muslim conference in Chicago with a few Muslim sisters, recently married Nicole told a hilarious story about a sister who regularly inquires about her marital status. Nicole retold, "*I only knew her by face but this sister would literally climb over stuff, people, whatever was in her way to come up to me and ask, 'Excuse me, is you Maaaarried?*'" Nicole held the word "married" for a good four seconds, with extra emphasis on the ending "d". As she told her story, we laughed at the audacity of this woman! Nicole could now look back at it with humor, but she remembered how hurt and disrespected she felt when the woman would ask that question. It was as if her single status was a weakness, something for people to point out to others. Though this experience was obviously a bit extreme, we laughed, both at Nicole's comical retelling, but also because on some level we all had similar stories.

Family members and community members who repeatedly inquire about marital status cause a lot of unwanted mental stress and to put it bluntly, single Muslims are tired of it! One brother recounted, "*My parents keep trying to get me married off, they wonder what's wrong with me.*" Another stated, "*I'm tired of hearing 'Oh wow, you're still single? But you're so nice. Isn't they anyone in your area?'*" One sister said, "*I hate it. I come to the masjid and this sister is like 'Oh, are you married?' When I said 'no' she cocked her head to the side and sighed, 'aww, that's too bad.' I mean come on, nobody wants to hear that all the time!*"

Muslim young adults who grow up in a family or culture that places a high value on marriage and children often feel conflict around their single status, especially post-college. In response to these types of experiences, single Muslims have begun to form support groups. One group on Facebook, a social-networking website is named *Happily Single in the Muslim Community (HSMC).* They list themselves as "A network advocating for equality and respect for single and/or unmarried Muslims, promoting their meaningful representation and participation in American Muslim communities, organizations, and Islamic Centers." The group serves as a place where Muslims who are in a period in life where they "do not desire considering marriage, can find affirmation and support for their temporary choice of a single lifestyle." Several member posts highlight the persistent, unwanted marital pressure.

I wanna be married, I just want my family to shut up about it!

> *Salaam* (greeting of peace)! How tired we all get of the question, "When are YOU getting married?" *Akhe* (brother), since my younger cousin got married my aunt always brings it up when I talk to her on the phone. I think this group is great. Personally, I am currently single by choice because this is just a bad time for me to get into a partnership. But whether someone has a partner or not shouldn't open them up to criticism, ostracism, or less respect. (Facebook Post #1 from brother)

Another post reads,

> My family is in a panic that I'm not married yet. Especially since my younger sister, and three younger cousins are married. It really is not in my control. A good guy is hard to find :((sad face) And I'm in no rush :) (happy face) Whatever happened to having faith in Allah that everything will work out for the best? (Facebook Post #2 from sister)

Every human is born single and shall at least remain single for least some part of their lives. So you may ask, if singlehood is a natural state of being, why is it sometimes deemed negatively? What causes the shift? Well, one answer is *age*. The most socially acceptable marital age range appears to be early 20's for women and mid-to-late 20's for men. Every year past that ideal range exposes a young Muslim to increased family and community pressure. Karima describes how her family and community feel about the ideal marital age:

> I think if you're single and say near your thirties, people talk and wonder why you're not married yet. Even my mom has said ideally she wants me engaged by the time I'm 25 (laughing). And in our [conservative Pakistani] communities with girls as young as 17, 18 getting married you are sending a message that marriage is very important, even more than education. You know the trend is still to marry young (in our community). So if you're older and not married you're different, you're not following the normal pattern. So don't we usually associate anything different as a bit strange and wrong, no ☺
>
> And then there's the guys! They're the worst! They reinforce this idea of "ideal age to marry." The first guy my parents set me up with said that. I think I must have expressed that I wasn't sure if I was ready for marriage, I felt young, etc. He assured me *(maybe he was trying to be nice but I didn't take it like that)*, that 21 was when girls usually got married, it was perfect timing. But there really is no perfect timing. It's whenever you're ready and find the right guy.

Societal expectations reveal gender differences. Muslim singles receive pressure to marry but the pressure is often exerted stronger and longer on women first. Not marrying at the "right" age, can be a scary circumstance for women who live in communities where men prefer younger women, often passing over older women. Conversely, as young men in the community grow older, they are seen as more mature and stable, more "marriageable."

INTERNALIZING THE SHAME

Being single can begin to feel like being unemployed in a house where everyone else is working – it becomes a mark of devaluation. After a while, single Muslims learn that displaying their single status may invite the label of being "desperate." Answering questions like "*So have you met anyone yet?*" for the millionth time can be humiliating. As a result, some singles do not take advantage of the few opportunities for single Muslims because of shame. For example, when asked if she would ever attend a singles' event, Nailah responded,

> I've never done that either. I have had issues about feeling ashamed to do that sort of thing, embarrassment. I think I'm [almost] over it now but I was ashamed to be single. To tell people I'm looking. To tell a guy I'm interested. A lot of stupid stuff.

In this day and age of romantic movies and "falling in love," American Muslim young adults, like most Americans, have been conditioned to believe that they will meet their soul mates randomly: maybe in a class, perhaps at the grocery store, or maybe at work. Then, after a period of time, they will marry this person and live happily ever after. Unfortunately when that does not happen, they sometimes begin to imagine that personal defects like personality and/or physical flaws may be preventing them from achieving marriage. Am I pretty/handsome enough? Am I religious enough? Do I have enough money? Am I doing enough to get a mate? In the end, many singles see themselves as the reason for their prolonged singleness. Again Nailah speaks,

> Why does something that seems so natural seem so hard for me in a way? I think I focus a lot of energy on other things. But I'll admit that I have not when it comes to marriage. So I'm trying to reorient myself.....I'm just trying to be prepared for the good that is ahead of me, marriage being high on that list.

Muslims' personal desire for marriage is strong enough without the added pressure from the community. Singles often feel as if it is their ultimate goal to get married, but unfortunately they also believe the Muslim community is not conducive to finding a spouse. In particular, several informants point to the spatial gendering of Muslim spaces as a major hurdle.

REFLECTIONS

For Single individuals: How do you feel your single status is perceived in your family and community? Why?

For Community members: Think deeply, how do you treat single individuals in your family and community? Could your comments be taken as more negative than positive?

6

Reason # 4: I Don't Know How To Talk To The Opposite Sex!

The only time we ever talked to Muslim girls while growing up were at the family or friend gatherings that our parents would organize, summer camp, Eid (Muslim Holiday). Not really at the masjid though. (Hakim, 28)

Walk into any *masjid* and one of the first things an outsider may notice is a separation of the sexes. While several studies including the works of Muslim feminists, have analyzed gendered space in relation to a differential of power between Muslim men and women (see McCloud 1995; Ahmed 1992; Schmidt 2004; Rouse 2004), gender studies of Muslim space rarely highlight a differential of power between the parent generation that controls the organization of the space and the younger generation that is often more accustomed to mixed-gender interaction. This section analyses the hegemonic practice of gender separation and the ways in which some Muslims resist this most salient mark of *masjids*.

Masjid leaders I spoke with roughly divide the physical setup of *masjids* into four categories:

1. **Total Separation** –Men and women enter through separate entrances as well as pray in separate prayer halls. Segregation extends into the communal spaces (halls, etc) as well as to any community event.

2. **Segregated Prayer with divider** – Men and women may or may not enter through the same door. They have separate prayer areas often delineated by a wall or other type of divider. While communal space is usually mixed, it ma or may not include spatial distance between men and women.

3. **Segregated Prayer without divider** - Men and women usually enter through the same main door and pray in one hall without any physical divider. Women continue to pray behind the men and communal space is also segregated.

4. **Segregated Prayer without divider / Non-Segregated communal space.** Men and women enter through the same door, pray in one hall with no wall or other physical divider. Communal space is mixed with free intermingling.

(Adopted from Dawud Walid, Executive Director of CAIR)

EXPERIENCING A STRICTLY GENDERED MOSQUE

Masjid Al-Hakim is an example of a *masjid* with total separation. The sisters and brothers enter through separate doors and the two sides of the *masjid* are completely gender segregated. A wall of dark tinted glass divides the *musala* (prayer hall), and the women listen to the *khutbah* (prayer sermon) over the PA system. Personally, coming from a *masjid* in which cross-gender interaction is the norm, I initially found this *masjid's* physical separation, which extends beyond prayer services and into the Islamic classes, dinners and social events, both physically and intellectually stifling. Though I could understand how separating the prayer may be more comfortable for women, especially when breastfeeding for example, I could not understand why social functions, like dinners or lectures would be separated. My biases began to surface, "*These same men and women who push for barriers in the masjid work in offices with members of the opposite sex, go to school with members of the opposite sex, and shop at Meijer with members of the opposite sex. Why the seemingly hypocrisy?*' But more relevant to this study, I wondered how single Muslims meet and interact with potential spouses within this gendered space?

Later, when I spoke with Saleema, a second-generation Pakistani-American, I was given an 'insider's perspective' of gender separation. In her view, many community pioneers attempted to recreate "back home" at the *masjid.* Saleema shared, "*I think they thought 'if women don't go to the masjid in Pakistan, why would we do anything different just because we're now in the US?' The thought never occurred to them that by moving to the United States, they should also change their customs.*" Saleema reminds us of an interesting point - American culture does not wash away the cultures of immigrants. Though immigrants may hybridize their behaviors, traces of their previous cultures remain.

A lot of Muslims are more comfortable with 'John and Lisa' at school and work than 'Muhammad and Ayesha' at the masjid

Saleema also raised another point - that the struggle of new immigrants to maintain their culture came with unexpected consequences. Firstly, many American Muslim women, including Saleema's mother, are highly educated and integrated in the larger American community. Often, these women resist importing the cultural values of 'back home' which may not value their educational statuses to the U.S. (Haddad et al 2006). Secondly, many *masjids* are attended by both immigrants of other nations (see D'Alisera's 2004 study of Sierra Leonean New Yorkers), as well as indigenous Muslims whose cultural views may not always correspond to those of the predominate immigrant groups, often South Asian and/or Arabs. Lastly, the parent generation neglected to predict how recreating 'back home' in America may adversely affect their children's relationship with their Muslim peers and *masjid.*

Saleema and other Muslim young adults raised in strictly gendered environments where it was taboo to be friends or to even converse with the opposite sex, often end up feeling anxious, nervous or "weird" around Muslims of the opposite sex. She states, "*I think a lot of us just didn't know how to talk to the Muslim boys, I mean we weren't really allowed to even sit by them and they came in separate doors."* Now post-college and working alongside men everyday, Saleema still has some ambivalence around Muslim males (except the few she interacted with at college).

Others recount how moving between Islamically gendered spaces and public non-gendered spaces, where mixed-gender interaction is normative, often facilitated stronger relationships with non-Muslims. As Tahira stated, a young Muslim woman may not be able to talk with "Muhammad" freely at the *masjid*, but she can talk to "John" at school all day long without any social consequences or taboo.

Brothers described the same problem. Nazir, a self-described semi-conservative Pakistani-American explains, *"I have a harder time talking to Muslim girls than I do with non-Muslim girls."* When I asked him to explain he continued, *"I've been trained to believe that talking to Muslims girls is wrong. If there's a Muslim girl around, you start hearing your parents and your Islamic school teacher."* The Islamic spaces Nazir traversed regulated mixed-gender interaction – in his case, it simply didn't exist.

In order to position oneself as a "good" Muslim and to receive social acceptance, members of the Muslim community often follow these gender prescriptions whether they agree with them or not.

Why segregate?

The practice of gender separation has both Islamic and cultural origins. Many Muslims point out that in the Qur'an, the Prophet Muhammad's (pbuh) wives were commanded to not interact with general society. Further, because the Prophet Muhammad's (pbuh) wives are seen as an example for Muslim women as a whole, many Muslims feel the directive should extend to *all* women.

> O wives of the Prophet! You are not like any of the other women. If you fear God, do not be complaisant in speech so that one in whose heart is a sickness may covet you, but speak honorably. Stay quietly in your homes and do not display your finery as the pagans of old did.
>
> And when you ask (his wives) for anything you want, ask them from before a screen. That makes for greater purity for your hearts and for theirs (Quran 33:32-33 & 53).

The practice of gender segregation is also tied to the concept of sexual desires between men and women. As I previously mentioned, social interaction, mixing and intermingling between unrelated men and women is regarded as potentially leading to immoral sexual activity. Temptations and desires may arise and due to Islam's prohibition on extramarital sex, some Muslims believe that unrelated men and women should have no contact with each other. Others view this focus on temptations rather than love of God as the major problem. My father would tell me, *"God says when two are gathered in his name, then He will be the third. You just make sure you are gathering in His name."* Again this brings to mind the *niyah filter* and checking to makes sure one's intentions are pure, as well as shifts in religiosity. Lastly, the practice is often more cultural than religious in nature. As Mirza put it, *"Most Pakistanis regardless of religion are against things like dating and kissing."*

The only way I meet Muslims of the opposite sex is outside of the masjid

Whatever the reasons behind the prohibition on mixed-gender interactions, several young Muslims have internalized feelings of guilt and ambivalence surrounding interactions with the opposite sex, Muslims in particular. As in my first visit to Masjid Al-Hakim, many find there is a learning curve upon entering a new *masjid.* Some time must be spent just getting to know the culture of the space and the new "rules" for appropriate interaction between men and women. For example, Suleiman, 25, is a graduate student living in an area with a small Muslim community. He is the only African-American at a predominately immigrant *masjid* and he happens to hold divergent opinions of gender separation. He says, *"It can be awkward because you don't know the proper greetings or how to properly address the opposite sex. Some are and (some) are not okay with talking or looking at each other."*

These circumstances lead many men and women to adopt the strategy of no-conversation. Rather than engage in a conversation which may later be deemed "un-Islamic" or inappropriate, many simply choose to remain "with their kind" in the *masjids.* Often times this strategy extends to Muslim interactions in non-Muslim spaces. Many Muslims who are more comfortable talking to Muslims of the opposite sex interpret this avoidance as disrespect. Sisters described feeling angry when they see Muslim brothers who do not speak to them, on campus freely conversing with non-Muslim women. "*Why don't they talk to us, it's like they are ashamed of us or something*" said Kelly, a White American aged 27.

Though lengthy, the following excerpt from Jamilah Karim's article on the construction of American Muslim identities includes an interesting retelling of a gender relations workshop held at a Muslim young adult conference. A Muslim sister asks, "*Why does it seem that Muslim men are afraid of Muslim women or that Muslim women are somehow not good enough for them?*" (Karim 2005:506).

> A male panelist answered, "*Fortunately, I don't feel like that. Alhamdulillah (praise be to God) my wife is Muslim. I don't see why anyone would feel like that.*" However, a female panelist had a different opinion, "*My husband is not Muslim. I wanted to marry a Muslim, but brothers in this community would not approach me at all. I know scores and scores of sisters who are educated, financially established, firmly rooted in their Islam, but brothers are reluctant to approach them.*" One brother tried to give the brothers' side: "*We have been raised to respect Muslim women, and we are afraid of approaching them in an improper way. A lot of times we just don't know how to approach.*" A male audience member added, "*It's easier to approach Christian women because they will do certain things that a Muslim woman wouldn't. A Christian girl would probably go to all kinds of places with you, but with a Muslim girl, you would have to have another person with you because they say Satan is the third party if a man and woman are alone.*" A woman sharply rejoined, "*Why are you approaching them differently? She is still a woman. I don't care what religion she is, she is also to be respected in the same manner. Why are you approaching the situation different if either is potentially supposed to be your mate?*"

> Sakinah commented: "*If brothers don't know how to approach sisters, why not have someone else, perhaps a parent or an imam, approach them on your behalf? Islamically, to maintain a sense of respect and dignity, a brother should approach her wali (usually a male family member who acts as an initial mediator between a woman and a potential partner, counseling the woman on whether the interested party meets her requirements). Also, a sister can make the*

> *first move and have her wali approach a brother on her behalf*" (Karim 2005:505-506, *emphasis is mine*).

Muslim young adults of my study raised several of the same points as those in Karim's workshop. They have been told what *not* to do, i.e. date, or have premarital sex, but they have not been told what *to* do. For example, is it o.k. to approach a man if you are interested in him? Is an intermediary always necessary or is personal contact o.k.? How do you know how to act if the rules change? All of these questions assume that individuals have a chance to meet. If young Muslims are often too scared or nervous to talk to each other about non-personal matters, talking to someone for the purpose of marriage is even more difficult. Several Muslims are beginning to change these environments.

REDEFINING GENDER INTERACTIONS.

Many Muslim young adults do not wish to continue the gendered practices of their parents. Isam, an Indian-American, is accustomed to mixed-gender interactions. He understands his parents' cultural values regarding a separation of the sexes, but is still hopeful for change in his Muslim community. He states, *"They (parent generation) will never let go. The only way change will come is when they die and we take over (laughing)"* Isam, 24. Though it may sound harsh to speak of the eminent deaths of parents, (I have been criticized for making similar statements), Isam uses humor to express his frustration over a *masjid* culture he believes does not foster community. As for now, many single Muslims are hybridizing gender interaction rules by crafting new spaces to build understanding and mutual respect between Muslim men and women.

These new environments often begin in college, a space where gender interaction is the norm. In particular, Muslim Students Associations (MSAs) often serve as alternate locations for gender interaction amongst Muslim young adults (Schmidt 2004). Growing from just 75 students in 1963, the MSA now boasts of hundreds of chapters in North America (www.msa-natl.org). Naturally, MSA's treat gender relations in a variety of ways, some are more strict than others. Still, for Muslim young adults who grew up in gender separated Muslim communities, MSAs often afford the first opportunity to freely interact with Muslims of the opposite sex.

For example, in California, I had the opportunity to befriend two members of an ethnically diverse MSA chapter. Every Friday night, about 10-12 active members hold a *halaqa* (Islamic study circle). Beginning at 7:00pm, the *halaqa*, taught by the host (an immigrant graduate student) lasts from one to two hours. After the lesson the group usually orders pizza and socialize and philosophize until roughly 1:00 or 2:00 a.m.. when I asked one member for his thoughts on the late hour, he responded, *"At least we're socializing with other Muslims and not out at the club!"*

During their lesson, men and women tend to sit on different sides of the carpeted floor but after the lesson, everyone is free to mingle and talk. The air is one of familiarity, with lots of teasing and practical joking - the members see themselves as true friends. Though not their primary goal, they also see the MSA as a great place to find a Muslim spouse. They have the opportunity to observe someone's manners in a relaxed Muslim environment. I personally know of several couples that have grown out of MSA environments.

For Nailah, college provided the first real encounter with Muslim men. She remembers, *"I was walking around at this restaurant. These two brothers from the MSA gave me salaams and one offered me some of his Belgian waffle. [laughing] Over the years, they became some of my closest friends."* Nailah is now 27 and based on her college experiences, her attitudes regarding gender separation have changed.

> We don't follow those rules anymore, the whole 'don't talk to brothers.' I can be at a gathering with non-Muslim men and women and we're talking about things so why shouldn't I do that with Muslim men and women. So I think it's hypocritical, and why should I do that? So if we want to have Muslim men over and we talk and get to know each other then that's what we do. We're creating bonds.

Nailah and her Muslim friends (male and female), now get together at each other's homes on a regular basis. However, Nailah feels it is unfortunate this group has yet to result in a marriage. According to her, their common singleness is still the "pink elephant in the room." She explains that often the friends do not want to "ruin what we have going by talking to someone. What if it doesn't work out?"

"STRICTLY BUSINESS" MIXED GENDER CONVERSATIONS

Not all young Muslims fight for interaction, or agree that men and women can be "buddies." For Layla, a Pakistani American, personal experience has shown that 'weird' feelings can arise when you get too close. While on a study abroad in the Middle East, she became friends with two American Muslim brothers and another Muslim sister. One of the young men, Israel, a real "Indiana Jones," proposed they all take a trip to Palestine, something that would normally fall outside of Layla's comfort zone.

> We were there for two weeks, staying with people and in random hostels. I think I decided I wouldn't let the whole gender thing hold me back from such an amazing opportunity. I just tried to keep it *halal* (permissible) as much as I possibly could. [laughing] We got very close because we were all starving together or being held at gun point by the Israelis so it was one of those experiences you never forget, the checkpoints are soooo scary.

The four college students continued their friendship throughout their study abroad. Now back home and once again in a gendered Muslim environment, Layla has a few regrets and wonders if the trip was a bad idea.

> I don't necessarily agree with the way I treated them (as brothers). They were too familiar with me, I think I should have just keep it business with guys, not necessarily have a heart attack, but just be cool about it and assertive. I mean I know it's o.k. to joke once in a while but I acted like Dave and Israel were my BUDDIES [laughing], I basically treated them like my girlfriends, I should have calmed down a little. Cause I think that in Islam there are certain ways of dealing with guys. ... I think in Islam you're supposed to keep it "business like." (Just) get what you need and then get out of there.

Layla is not alone. Other informants find gender segregation ideal or simply no cause for alarm. For example, Nazir, who grew up in a strictly gendered *masjid*, stated, "*I guess I just never said to myself 'Gee, I wish there were sisters at this [masjid] dinner.' I never really paid any attention to it. But I guess if there was some type of community event, maybe (gender integration) would be more important.*" The only time Nazir thought about women was during class when he realized it was a bit difficult for women to ask a question behind tented glass.

For Najee, the lines between appropriate and inappropriate behaviors are also more blurred. She approves of hanging out in group settings but believes women should not hang out with *non-mahram* (men she could legally marry) alone. She states, "*You're supposed to have respectful professional relationships with your male colleagues and friends.*"

And now that Fatima is older and in college, the definition of "respectful" has changed. She is very in-tune with her religious boundaries and does not try to cross them. Her parents seem to have changed as well.

> Now I can call up a guy or talk to them on the Internet and it's not weird because my personal beliefs and my personal line for what's appropriate and how to act with boys is very close to my mother's ideas and beliefs. So I don't think it bothers her if I do call up a guy from school. Maybe she's liberaled out a bit, maybe she sees me as a woman and not as a little girl who can do something foolish without thinking or knowing what the consequences will mean. I drive home guys to Chicago and stuff (from college) and my parents don't seem to mind (which in my eyes is uncharacteristic with what we were taught as kids) but either they've changed, or the rules have changed or having someone drive you home is an exception. I guess the rules have changed, they have to a bit with time and needs.

Fatima's story highlights the shifting nature of appropriateness depending both on the context as well as intentions behind the act. Because she was simply riding home from college, the rule against being in close proximity with a man alone was relaxed.

Gender interactions are very important in any community. It appears that for some, the strict gender separation of all things/events in many Masjids is difficult to handle. The contrast between Muslim spaces and other spaces is sharp.

REFLECTIONS

How are gender relations handled in your masjid or community space? Why? Has it affected how you view the opposite sex?

7

Reason # 5
I Need a B.A., Money And/Or Career Before I Marry

Most Muslim young adults want to get married at some point in their lives. However like everyone, the questions posed are, "When to get married? Who to marry? And how do I find that person?" Beginning with the first question of when to get married, education (for women and men), and money (for men) are the two most commonly quoted pre-requisites for Muslim young adults to seriously consider marriage. A third less common response would be personal development and/or career.

Education

Many parents see the value of having a college education in today's economy and as such, the pursuit of education is accepted as a justifiable reason to delay marriage. For social and economic advancement, many Muslims complete at least a bachelors (and increasingly higher education degrees) before marriage (a trend also documented in studies of American singlehood (DePaulo 2006; Stein 1975). Take Nadia for example, who says, *"I always knew I would get married after I finished my bachelors because that's what my parents always told me, so I never sat down and planned my wedding in my head. I (now) think more about life after marriage, which is so weird…how life would change."*

In another case, Layla's parents were also pretty firm about "no marriage license without at least a bachelor's degree (for both parties)." When her sister Lameena tested their resolve by first finding a boyfriend on her own and second, accepting his marriage proposal, her parents did not agree. Though he was Muslim and South Asian, her parents said they must finish school first. Layla agrees with their decision.

> I agree with my parents. You should have a degree or at least be in some sort of a program so that you have some way of supporting yourself later on. I wouldn't want my daughters getting married right out of high school. And even with my sister I agree with my mom making her wait because she was just flopping around in college, trying on different fields/careers. I think it's good that she knew she had to focus a bit and figure out what she wants to do (teach) and GET INTO a program before my parents take this seriously. It all depends on your situation, how focused you can be, is school going to take you apart (different cities), will you be able to handle that?

Marriage does not prevent an individual from attending and completing school. I do not mean to belittle the life changes and responsibilities that come with marriage, or that having a child can make it difficult to finish a higher education degree. But parents who prevent their children from marrying early do not appear to evaluate the impact of dating and other relationships on schooling. Like marriage, dating and romantic relationships can also capture the energy of students. Early marriages could serve as a solution to navigating the sex cultures. If married in college, they would not only be able to focus on school, but also be able to engage in Islamically agreeable sexual activity.

MONEY

The second pre-requisite for marriage mostly pertains to Muslim men and it concerns the means to support and protect a wife. The Quran states,

> Men shall take full care of women with the bounties which Allah has bestowed more abundantly on the former than on the latter, and with what they may spend out of their possessions (Qur'an 4:34).

A Muslim husband bears the financial responsibility for clothing, feeding and sheltering. The wife has no obligation to contribute to the family expenses unless she has the means and the desire to do so. According to Islamic law, this is a legally enforceable duty that is required for a period of time, even in the event of divorce. As a result, Muslim young men often must wait to get married until they have the means to support their wife. A typical undergraduate income living on student loans would not be able to bear this responsibility. For example, Ali thought he would get married at age 23. However, when that time came, neither his financial status nor marriage mentality were ready for a wife. He also blames Muslim women's material requirements.

> Most Muslim girls, man the standards are high. I was hanging around a bunch of Muslim women and they seemed like they wanted a perfect man. Which I am obviously not. Who knows (what the perfect man is). I know Muslim girls are hella materialistic so you have to have a lot of money to even think about it. Especially these urban college educated women. They have standards of living their parents gave them. They have been coddled so it's intimidating. I am being honest. It's hard to figure out how to buy a house, a car, etc. and stay in a city that has some soul. If I marry one of these younger sisters that has been "raised right" then I have to have a HUGE bank account. And they are so rigid! Islamically, life experience wise. I feel like I could not be my full self. They want some virgin man, some moneyed man, someone that will do what they say as well. In many ways they are as bought into the feminist ethic as non-Muslim women

Whether realistic or not, Ali certainly felt that without money, marriage to a Muslim woman would be impossible. While Ali's view of women is correct in some cases, most Muslim women do not expect a mansion with marriage. In fact, they often focus on the characteristics and potential of the man versus his bank account. As we shall see later, money may not be the huge obstacle young men think it is.

While Mirza is not as critical of Muslim women as Ali, money has also served as the major obstacle in his fulfilling his dream of getting married.

> Of course (I want to get married). I feel like I've been ready for a while but there are sometimes obstacles that get in the way of this readiness. For example, I knew I couldn't actually get married in college because I wouldn't want to rely on my parents financially. So I thought if I could get a good financial aid package and a TA job in grad school, then I could support a wife, that was the plan.

This burden to provide is a huge part of a man's life. Even when women contribute, they often feel it is their job to bring home the bacon (beef of course!). Again, the "letter to the brothers" in the appendix addresses these types of issues further.

CAREER

Increasingly, young Muslims are also delaying marriage in order to become settled in their careers. Marriage is sometimes seen as the old "ball and chain" and individuals should do as much "fun" stuff as they can before marrying. When I asked Nailah why many Muslims delay marriage she responded,

> I think we have gotten caught up in the material things in this world and have become selfish. I think we have figured that marriage is a hindrance so we have to do as much as possible before getting married, so it will be less likely that marriage can ruin our plans. ... and as Muslims, if you think you can hold on to your chastity for long enough then marriage is not too pressing. But then we are fooling ourselves.

Nadirah, the young woman who has not yet decided if she will be Muslim or not, is an example of Nailah's statement. She has decided that there is too much she wants to do right now to be concerned with marriage.

> I want to get comfortable in my new life first…I want to move and start my career…I don't need extra baggage. I want to get married around 26. Well actually nowadays relationships are as close as you can get to marriage (laughing)

I asked Nadirah to explain what she means about relationships being close to marriage. She responded, "*People do the same things in a relationship as if they were married. That's why a lot of men just wanna shack up (laughing). Why buy the cow if you can get the milk for free?*" Nadirah's statement reiterates literature, which highlights the decline of marriage in response to the wide availability of activities (sex and economic freedom) which were once classified as "marital behaviors" (Stein 1975; DePaulo 2006).

No Money + No Degree = No Marriage

Others like Hakim, an African-American male, want to delay their marriages until they have completed their Islamic studies and made the pilgrimage to *hajj*. He feels like a wife may detract him from accomplishing those goals. For those who have a degree, money and career, there is still one thing they must do before they can get married: find a spouse.

REFLECTIONS

For Singles: Are there any internal or external forces holding you back from marriage? If yes, what are they?

For community members: What stipulations have you placed on the marriages of your children and fellow community members? Why?

8

Reason # 6
I Have High Expectations

Well marriage is something that I've sort of been looking forward to for a while now. I mean people make all sorts of plans but what ends up happening is by the will of Allah. You know as they say man proposes and God disposes. So to be honest, my plan was to already be married once I started grad school. I had these lofty visions of being a married grad student and thought how cool that would be…just supporting each other as a young couple. Only one problem, I didn't find the girl lol. So you know, although I'm kind of anxious, I've sort of come to grips with reality. (Mirza, 22)

Mirza's quote above indicates how many respondents felt. They are ready to marry but unable to find a spouse. While Islam itself provides guidance on how to *choose* a spouse, many wanted specific prescriptions on how to *find* that person. The Prophet Muhammad is reported to have said, "Men choose women for four reasons: for their money, for their rank, for their beauty and for their religious character. So marry one who is best in religion and you will succeed" (Bukhari, Muslim). Muslims (men and women) are encouraged to consider a mate's religiosity first, and other qualities second. Also, the Quran states, "Women of purity are for men of purity, and men of purity are for women of purity" (Quran 24:26), indicating that virgins should marry other virgins. Other verses pertain to religious requirements. The following verse is often interpreted to mean that Muslim men are able to marry Muslim women as well as "people of the book," most commonly described as Christians and Jews.

> Also, you may marry the chaste women among the believers, as well as the chaste women among the followers of previous scripture, provided you pay them their due dowries. You shall maintain chastity, not committing adultery, nor taking secret lovers. Anyone who rejects faith, all his work will be in vain, and in the hereafter he will be with the losers (Quran 5:5).

The predominant view regarding spousal selection for women is that Muslim women should marry Muslim men only. This is based on the following verse,

> … and give not your daughters in marriage to idolaters till they believe, for a believing slave is better than an idolater though he please you. These invite unto the Fire, and Allah invite you unto the Garden, and unto forgiveness by His grace, and expound His revelations to mankind that they may remember (Quran 2:221).

Although lately there is some dissension amongst Muslims in reference to the correct interpretation of this verse, the popular view remains that marriage amongst Muslim women and non-Muslim men is *haram* (not permissible).

At a minimum, these are the most commonly understood Islamic prescriptions on marriage. However, naturally every individual has personal preferences in regards to appearance, personality and family background. Next, I explore some of the responses given in regards to what single Muslim men and women are looking for in a spouse.

WHAT A MUSLIM MAN DESIRES IN A WIFE

A Beautiful Muslima

While it is Islamically and socially acceptable for Muslim men to marry non-Muslim women, all of my informants stated they prefer to marry Muslim women (though they don't always know how to talk to them). Mirza, for example, has been anticipating getting married for quite some time and is actively searching for his mate. He is very clear about the type of young *Muslima* he would like to marry.

> Fundamentally, I'm looking for a partner in the path towards paradise – in other words, a sister whose number one priority in life is Islam. A practicing *muslima* who is in tune with her purpose in life and is zealous about following her faith and someone who tries to implement the Qur'an and Sunnah of the Prophet Muhammad (pbuh) in everyday life. I prefer someone who wears *hijab*. Beyond that, I guess I have a bunch of secondary preferences, doesn't everybody? I prefer someone who is down to earth and easy to talk to. Also someone who likes to discuss Islam, someone with good character and a sense of humor too!

Though Nazir, also a Pakistani-American begins his list with beauty, he too desires a Muslim woman.

> Well I'd like to be physically attracted to her. I know that sounds shallow, and in the long run it doesn't matter, but for me it's important. Which doesn't mean she has to be a supermodel or anything, I just have to be attracted to her, even if everybody else in the world thinks she's hideous. Second is I want her to be a pious woman. I'd like her to be religious and I'd also like to get to a point where my first priority is her piety and everything else secondary. Unfortunately, I'm not at that point yet. And if she can cook, that's a huge plus because the only thing I can make is pasta (laughing).

For Ali, the young man who went through a major spiritual transformation, the choice is not that simple.

> I've been looking for what I call a Doomsday Girl. A woman that when the world is ending, I do not want to be anywhere else. She needs to be adept in the country and the city. Needs to be able to shit in the woods (sorry for the expletive), tend plants, and heal wounds in case I had

> to go off and fight or die. (I want) the kind of woman that would make certain that any kids we had would never go hungry: spiritually or physically.

Ali's ex-girlfriend was his Doomsday girl until he realized that she was perfect in every way, except that "*her relationship with Allah is lacking.*"

> I guess it's that she defers to secular explanations of things and science over the Quran. She sees the Quran as a book of stories. She has not really investigated it from what her parents taught her. And they were not very religious at all. There's no perfect woman it seems, I just need to make a choice.

Ali sees Leila's positions as a product of the times including feminism. He also believes women are writing their own script when it comes to relationships, and that script is too heavily based on the unrealistic and untruthful messages of popular culture.

> I blame feminism and the whole secular cult that wants women to be in competition with men on almost every level. Think about it, think about all your independent friends, about the emasculation of men and liberal enlightenment that separated man's law from God's law and took the divine out of our relationships. They needed to do that to enslave people, to do the colonial project. And now, we are totally disconnected from ourselves, God, and nature. Roles have no meaning. Secular society puts us equal to animals so then sex is a sport. Men and women have no roles so women are trying to prove equality when that does not exist. We are not equal, we have our special characteristics. Look at the popular movies that we also laugh at. Look at how men are portrayed as shiftless, as lazy, as sex obsessed. We play into that as well and women are portrayed as victims. Group think is the way that we are not independent thinking, not thinking as Muslims, not being critical of the whole framework of our arguments. For example, sisters always talk about men who ain't worth much, who do not have

> the same level of education, it's like a broken record they have been hearing and are repeating. Chris Hedges said this: part of the problem is people who create a morality based on their own experience, which is what of course the New Atheists and the Christian fundamentalists have done. Feminism is the perfect example of that principle.

Muslim young adults are critically analyzing the state of our society and the root causes of social ills like a weakening of marriage institutions, as well as problems finding a spouse. In turning to Islam for guidance and solutions, they are changing how religion functions in a society.

Elijah, an African-American 36-year-old professor likes to engage in philosophical discussions like Ali, but this time his discussion of Muslim women and his singleness was on a much more basic level. Having tried several outlets to meet a wife, including online matrimonial services, through school, and work, until recently, he was just unable to meet his dream wife.

> Either I met someone I really liked but the whole Arab/Desi culture clash thing (*see the section on endogamy below for more discussion on this issue*) or, with people from my own background they just didn't have their stuff together. Some were really pushy up front like, "*Hi. My name is so-and-so. Let's get married tonight*" (laughing). Or they'd drag it out for weeks without any pics, very hesitant to show pics like pics are *haram* or something. And then of course, I see the pic, and the sister isn't very attractive and then people's feelings get hurt because they get attached.

I'm looking for a Doomsday girl …one who can make certain our kids would never go hungry, spiritually or physically - Ali

Like Nazir, Elijah is very open about the fact that physical appearance is important to him. However, one woman was a bit too revealing. Elijah revealed, "*Some sister sent me butt naked pics after just two emails….Totally outrageous!!*" The woman was on the *da'wah* committee (the committee that goes out to invite people to learn about Islam). Elijah joked, "*Brothers will definitely be takin' shahadah (becoming Muslims).*"

Over the years, quite a few women have approached Elijah for marriage, he believes in part because he speaks Arabic. As another brother said, "*Muslim men who appear to be strong Muslims are a hot commodity.*" Still, I wondered, within the 18 years Elijah has been Muslim, not ONE woman was wife material? Elijah then revealed the deeper reason he is still single, "*I'm very choosy, not like cats (men) who jumped in not knowing who they were or what they were looking for.*" Elijah knows exactly what he wants in a wife and is unwilling to compromise on those aspects. For one, Elijah is very keen on *hijab:*

> (I want a wife that) COVERS, not the lamp shade *hijabi.* I don't mean *niqab* (veil). I don't care for any of that, but you know what I'm talkin' about: sisters that wear a head wrap like Badu but still walk around with the front exposed; the *hijab* ain't never really on tight. I prefer *hijab.* If the sister isn't ready to cover like it's meant to be done, may Allah guide her...but naw, that ain't for me. Yeah, I'm old school. She can dress modestly...doesn't have to be in an abaya and all but again, what's the point if I can see your form, all laid out with nothing left to the imagination, and still front with *hijab*?

For Elijah, (and he would say in Islam), there are specific rules regarding the way a woman should cover her body, sometimes including everything except her face, hands and feet. By "lamp shade *hijabi*" and "head wrap" like the R&B singer Erykah Badu, Elijah is referring to a Muslim woman who wears a scarf on her head but exposes her neck, which Ali sees as contradictory to the purpose of hijab. We laughed because Elijah's description of the "head wrap *muslima*" fit me perfectly, thank God my husband doesn't feel the same way!

While these are clearly personal choices, Elijah's response about *hijab* is telling. For many people, *hijab* represents a level of understanding within Islam – it is an outward expression of an inner faith. Remember Tahira who wore her *hijab* in a less "*muslimy*" way when she was involved in activities that could be deemed un-Islamic. A woman who wears *hijab* is often assumed to be more knowledgeable about Islam than her non-*hijab*i counterparts. Yet, a piece of cloth can never fully represent the level of a sisters' personal commitment to God. So you may have someone who lives their life as a Muslim but chooses to not cover their hair. Still, *hijab* is a deal breaker for some men. Their fellow sisters suggest they look deeper to the heart of the person, as one sister stated, *"I know several niqabis (women who wear a face veil) who got knocked up, that shouldn't be their (brothers') focus."*

Suleiman

Suleiman grew up in a variety of cities and cultural environments, and his life experiences are reflected in what he is looking for in a spouse. His father has always pushed him to marry a "beautiful righteous *hijabi*," but his preferences are a bit looser.

> I prefer a *muslima* that's not too serious but striving on her *deen*. That loves me, is intelligent in both worldly and religious knowledge and attractive. Arabic is not required for me, but I certainly see it as a bonus.

Suleiman is also leaning towards an interracial marriage and has thought about how a different family background may enhance his life.

> I dunno, the older I get the more I think that it makes sense to be with someone of the same culture; but my eyes are drawn to women from all over the world. I see a lot that I like in an international spouse like extension and global relationships. A cultural enrichment/infusion into the family. Giving your children a broader perspective, like how Obama's experience benefits him.

Unfortunately, Suleiman now lives in an area where there are three strikes against him: 1) he is new to the Muslim community; 2) there are very few Muslim sisters; and 3) there is no interaction between the sisters and brothers. He explained the gender relations,

> There are no, single *muslimas* here. Most men keep their wives at home inside all day until they get there and then they walk around campus together. That's it, so I don't want to offend any sisters or their husbands by talking etc. It can be awkward because you don't know the proper

> greetings or how to properly address the opposite sex. Some people are and some people are not okay with talking or looking at each other.

Gender separation also organizes the social events. Suleiman gave the example of a community BBQ. While sisters attend, they are separated on the women's side of the *masjid* "by several walls and locked doors." When I laughed at the thought of going through several walls and locked doors, Suleiman said, *"You laugh but it's true. I cook the meat and we send plates over to the sisters' side."* Suleiman estimates 70% of the mostly immigrant men are single, *"Most of the brothers all go back to India or Jordan to get married because there are none here. The closest place to find sisters about 40min east of here into Texas."* In response to his situation, Suleiman has thought about ways to find a spouse.

> I can try a conversion move like some brothers do; or use the Muslim websites to find someone; or talk to brothers and see who they can hook me up with. One brother did hook me up with a sister in Egypt. She's very nice, but young and really wants to stay in Egypt.

Suleiman has been talking to this sister over the internet for a little while but doesn't think they will get married. He has reflected on the type of woman he wants, but is not certain he will be able to find her.

> I want a wife, but I'm not sure what I really really want. I don't really wanna revert someone using the relationship as pressure. My family hasn't made any really efforts to do anything, they just kinda threaten me every now and then with the arranged marriage bit...and it's something that I'm not even opposed to. It's just getting harder and harder to do the right thing, especially out here.

Though they all had personal preferences, the brothers of this study were clear that they want to marry a Muslim wife. The fact that they are open to marriage but have not been able to find a spouse is telling. Many assume that singlehood for men is easier than for women because they are the "hot commodity." They have the option to choose whoever they want. We see here that it is not that simple, finding a Muslim wife is not as easy as pie and many single brothers are left wondering what to do.

WHAT A MUSLIM SISTER DESIRES IN A HUSBAND

An Educated, Egalitarian who is not Afraid of Housework

Muslim women described wanting men who are compassionate, loving, generous, religious and accepting. Most often, they wanted a man who held similar values as them and were egalitarian in their views. For example, women who remained chaste want to marry a man who is also a virgin. Aliyah states, "*I prefer a virgin. I don't want a man who has been all around and then decided to settle down and get married. Why should he get me after I've been struggling to do good all this time. Uh uh, I want a virgin man.*"

I'm a virgin and I want a virgin man too.

Fatima, a Pakistani-American is very concerned about finding a spouse that is sensitive and egalitarian in his beliefs, traits she thinks many traditional Pakistani men do not carry.

> I would LOVE it if just once I asked a guy hypothetically, "*if I was making more money than you and one of us had to stay home and I said I would like to keep working, would you mind being at home with the kids*" and he said "*Yes.*" ☺ (laughing) But let's be honest, if that was my criteria, I'd never get married ☺. There are some things growing up here you just become. Like I'm independent and I want to be an equal. I guess I borrow, I mesh, I blend, I pick and choose (from my cultures). I know our culture is very family orientated so yes, I'm willing to live in an extended family. I'm willing to treat your parents as my own. But as an American I'm used to this idea of "*respect me too if you want to be respected*" so I would expect him to treat my parents the same way. If they need someone to take care of them, I will/we will. I don't think I can marry a South Asian. I

> know South Asian men and I've already told my mom please try to find me an ABCD ☺ not that they all suck. My cousin, her husband is Pakistani and she is just as Americanized if not more Americanized than me.

Initially I was confused by what Fatima meant by a South Asian man, seeing that she herself is South Asian. She explained she was referring to someone who grew up "back home" and that an "ABCD" is an American-Born Confused Desi (A South Asian American). Like Fatima, Saleema also desires an ABCD, *"I guess I want to marry the male version of me, a Pakistani man who grew up here in America. Who likes having fun and doesn't mind a professional wife."* However, now that she has graduated from college and there are no outlets for meeting Muslim men in her community, she worries if she will ever find a husband and is trying to prepare herself for the possibility that she may never marry.

I want an ABCD – an American-Born Confused Desi, just like me!

Spirituality was also important for a husband. One Pakistani-American 24-year-old indicated,

> I am looking for a spiritual Muslim. By that, I mean I don't really agree with the term religious sometimes because the connotation is that someone who prays 5 times a day, fasts, etc. But I'd ideally like someone who really desires to further a connection to God, Islam, etc in their heart. They read books, articles, go to lectures, be an active Muslim, but in the end, really really feel it and believe it. And someone I can improve my faith with together.

Money, Money, Money

There is a myth that all Muslim women care about marrying someone with a lot of money. As a woman who married a PhD student on a student's salary, I know from experience that is not true. But I will admit, some women do have unrealistic expectations. When I chatted with Nadia, a 22-year-old Pakistani American about marital preferences she stated:

> I think we are very unrealistic in our expectations of partners. For girls and parents of the girl, when they look, they always want a guy who is making a lot of money (doctor, lawyer, engineers, dentist and in that order). And if anything less, they will look elsewhere. For guys, they want us as housewives, beautiful and someone they can show. The real concept of marriage is left behind to have a person who would stick with you through and through, with good religious and moral values.

Though she critiques the idea, Nadia raises the point of parental expectations and explains that she too has adopted these preferences, *"You know those are becoming my personal preferences, my parents will not accept anything else so I have to pretty much agree to the same."* Even in the age of individualism, family preferences often trump personal choice for many young Muslims. Nadia's statements are examples of the ways tradition become *doxa,* or the natural order of things (Maira 2002). Young adults often preserve the cultural purity of their parents by adopting their parents' views of "moral authority." The traditions become "incarcerated in the *doxic* prison of innocence (Brow 1990:3 in Maira 2002:52). As Nadia reveals, she will accept her parents' preferences as her own in order to maintain kinship and ethnic ties.

For Nadirah, the young lady who wants to delay marriage until she is settled into her career, goals and ambition appear to be high on her list:

> I want someone who isn't lazy, someone that understands me and who wants the best things for me, someone who is up for change. Someone who is sweet and giving and loves his family, someone who HAS GOALS, I'm not taking care of anyone. Some men have an ego problem if I make more than them… but I want someone who has a career. Of course, I don't want a broke man. Money does mean something to me because I'm a brat (laughing). It really doesn't matter if he makes a little less than me but he can't just be lazy and laying on the couch playing video games. But you know most men want to make more…and if they have a woman who makes more than them it makes them wanna get out and try to do something better.

There exists a stigma on single Muslim men: that Muslim men who are not married simply choose to be single. Because there are more single women than men (though narrowly), women feel singlehood for men should be easy. For example, when I spoke to Tahira about a single man I knew, she asked,

> What's wrong with him? He must be looking for something very particular because a Muslim man doesn't have to be single if he doesn't want to be. There are single sisters everywhere. When men start having particulars that is what holds you up (laughing). Maybe I am biased (laughing).

I tried to present the brothers side, that many obstacles prevent men from marrying like being unknown in the community and not having enough financial resources. However, Tahira shot those ideas down.

> Please! There are women who would marry if you don't have the funds. Shoot, I would marry someone without the funds as long as they were being proactive to get there!

I asked if she would really consider someone who was broke but with "potential." She responded, *"Yea! That's what I was trying to say, I am tired (laughing)! As long as they are working towards being able to have the funds. I can't deal with broke and no work ethic or ambition lol."* Many Muslim women like Tahira are more interested in ambition and the promise of a beautiful life together than finances. They are willing to accept that they must build a life together prior to having the house and mansion. However, with the seemingly narrow pool of eligible Muslim men, Muslim women are stepping into new territory.

"Convertibles" Marrying non-Muslims

I mentioned earlier the majority of Muslims adhere to the understanding that it is prohibited for a Muslim woman to marry a Muslim man. Therefore, it is shocking to discover that one of the most interesting trends regarding mate preferences for some single Muslim young adult women is their openness to marry a non-Muslim man. In fact, three sisters explained their change of heart.

Zahra is a 27-year-old psychologist. She converted to Islam from Christianity and is the only Muslim in her family. She loves Islam but finds it a struggle to stay within the boundaries of Islamic singlehood. Her relationships with men have been “interesting.”

> I can't seem to get a Muslim brother to pay me attention for anything. (laughing) All of the sisters in the community say it is because the pickings are slim up here. *shrugs* I wanted to marry a Muslim but I was wondering where I was going to find one. Especially if I decide to return to the South after school. That means that I am going back to the Bible belt. I was thinking that I may have to import a brother from the North or Atlanta or something (laughing).

"Drop top" = A good man that I can convert to Islam - Tahira

While Muslim men do not approach Zahra, she receives a lot of attention from non-Muslims.

> I tend to attract conservative, yet open-minded Christians and the "conscious" brothers, regardless of religion. At first, I said, "no dating...no dating...good Muslim...no dating..." but coming from where I come from, that was very, very hard. So I date. I have my Muslim friends check him out, though (laughing).

Zahra thinks her appearance, (she usually dons a headwrap and a long skirt), is what attracts the “conscious brothers and Christians.” She now has a 27-year-old boyfriend, Michael, that she really likes even though he has other things, “career and education”, that he needs to work out before they can marry. Spiritually, Michael was from the Church of God in Christ but he eventually left them. He is now considering Islam.

> He had been taking the spiritual route for the longest, but started studying Islam before he met me. He keeps talking about taking his *shahadah* (becoming Muslim). I just want him to do it for the right reasons. Even if he does, I could still see him being "spiritual but not religious".

Zahra says she is "pretty serious" about this relationship and there is an 80% chance she and Michael will marry. I asked her how she envisions her future marriage and what qualities drew her to her boyfriend, she responded:

> I see our marriage as being a happy one. The intellectual discourse is great. I have learned a lot from him because he associates with more of a diverse group of people than I do. Our families are different so it has been interesting learning from him. His qualities: patient, understanding, faithful (he made a vow never to cheat in a marriage or a relationship because his father was not faithful to his mother and he saw the effect it had on her), family oriented, intelligent, driven, good work ethic.

Zahra appreciates the differences in religions right now but it worries her that he does not always understand her rituals.

> Some things that I tell him about rituals in Islam (i.e. the lamb sacrifice at Eid (Muslim holiday)), he doesn't understand. He wonders why the sacrifices have to be made, why Muslims circle the kabba a certain number of times, what is so great about Zamzam water, etc. Because of these rituals, he tries to put us on the same page as Catholics, and wonders where the spirituality is behind these acts.

Not finding the Muslim man of her dreams, Zahra was forced to keep her options open and consider non-Muslim men. One may assume that Zahra's situation is unique or limited to converts without a Muslim family. However, Tahira grew up in a Muslim household and is extremely active in the Muslim community. Yet, she too has run into the same problem of finding a good Muslim man, and she too is considering marrying a non-Muslim man.

> I need a man (laughing). I was just considering going back to the "drop top" plan this weekend. In the last year and half I have met the craziest Muslim men. "Drop top" = convertible, i.e. non-Muslims (laughing). That's me and my

> friends code. I try not to but it's always the temptation. My neighborhood is full of beautiful convertibles who want to shower me with praises (laughing). Sometimes you just need some attention as a female but Insha'Allah (God Willing) I try to stay away.

Tahira is a Muslima whose interactions with Muslim men have just not worked out. However, for Aminah, interactions with Muslim men have been extremely painful. Aminah lives in fast-paced Los Angeles and is a former print journalist. Because of her job, other Muslims often perceive her to be a "party girl," someone who is not serious about Islam and "probably" sexually experienced. She wants to get married, but is facing a few obstacles.

> I'm looking to get married, it's just that there are so many non-Muslim men that I'm attracted to. But really, Muslim guys are so not interested in me (even though) I cover, I'm in the community, etc. They know my family. I'm not a random person. Everyone knows I was a journalist and they think I hang with the "stars' and that I travel all the time. They don't think my former lifestyle was Islamic (people have many opinions about me traveling alone, etc.) I really think I'm not Muslim enough for these folks.

I want to marry a Muslim Man but they seem to act like I'm kryptonite - Aminah

Aminah described one particularly trying courtship experience. When she met a Muslim man for dinner "the guy walked away after five minutes because my scarf wasn't proper." Aminah's date, like my informant Elijah, held particular *hijab* preferences. Ironically, the incidence also shows how the young man himself hybridizes Islam. He was on a "date", something others could have also viewed as un-Islamic. Instead of acting with respect and compassion for another human, the man left Aminah stunned, embarrassed and disappointed.

> These guys make you feel bad because you're not Hafiz (someone who has memorized the Quran). Or if you

> haven't memorized Bukhari (book of *Hadiths*) you're just not serious. You should hear them! If you are not a scholar, they reject you. But then they go and marry a Christian woman….I began to resent Muslim men.

These interactions with Muslim men have caused Aminah much hurt and pain. Like Zahra and Tahira, she is "tired of being lonely" and feels like she almost has no choice but to marry a non-Muslim man.

> I want to marry a Muslim man! But they act like I am kryptonite. I feel like I have no choice, sometimes I think I'm not trying hard enough, but I'm around, and available …. Everyone knows my family, my cousin works in the *masjid.* I mean, I want to be part of the community, but I know if I marry a non-Muslim man, it's a wrap. Kiss the community goodbye. I know sisters who are not in the community because they married non-Muslims.

Like Zahrah, Aminah now has a non-Muslim semi-boyfriend whom she would consider marrying. They are great friends and Aminah enjoys his company. Given Aminah's preference for a Muslim man, I inquired about the seriousness of their relationship. She feels as if she is backed into a corner between her desire for intimacy, a serious relationship, and her desire to be a part of the Muslim community.

> I wish (he would propose). I think he's scared of me because I'm Muslim…not scared of me, but scared that I will not take our relationship seriously because he's not Muslim. The non-Muslim men think I am untouchable because I'm Muslim. And the Muslim men think I am not Muslim enough. I would love to marry him, but who would marry us? These *Imams* do NOT marry women to non Muslim men... I've seen it over and over and these mixed couples then get married at city hall and are ostracized from the community... no community for their kids, etc. I want to get married at the *Masjid.*

Social desirability is a big part of marriage and family life and being a part of the Muslim community is very important to Aminah. She states,

"I'm not the best Muslim, but I'm proud to be a Muslim and I would love an Islamic wedding." Zahra, Tahira and Aminah describe situations which have the potential to dramatically change the fabric of the American Muslim community. While some of their husbands may indeed convert to Islam, it is reasonable to assume that not all will. These inter-religious marriages would contribute to the ways in which the masjids and other religious institutions organize around marriage and family. In addition, it would be interesting to track the development of the children of these marriages.

Am I religious enough?

Lastly, like Amina, others recounted that Muslim brothers do not perceive them to be "Muslim enough." When Fatima was 20, her parents began to look for a spouse for her. Though she was not yet ready, she decided to go along with the program. She met someone she liked but the relationship ended before marriage.

> My parents started looking about two years ago, I met this one guy that I really hit if off with. We got to know each other a bit, then he decided he wanted to marry a hijabi (woman who wears a scarf) and I wasn't religious enough (☺) it was a slap in the face, laughing. Okay so then you know I get back up, dust myself off, remind myself that I'm a great Muslim no matter what he thinks and he can start by growing a beard! (laughing)

Fatima's last statement about "growing a beard" is a joke. For many conservative Muslims, Pakistani's included, a beard on a man is akin to a hijab on a woman. Apparently, Fatima's "fiancé" did not wear a beard, and therefore had no right to judge her because she did not wear a scarf.

REFLECTIONS

What makes a good spouse? Why? What makes a person undesirable for marriage? Why?

9

Reason # 7: I Need Help Finding A Spouse

(When the Aunties are not doing their job! - Aisha)

Asalamu alaikum warahmatullahi wabarakatuhu

InshaAllah (SWT) this email reaches you in the best health and iman. I am going to be blunt. I have been looking to get married for almost a year now with absolutely no success. I want it to be as Halal as possible and following the Sunnah of our beloved Prophet (SAW). The reason I'm sending this email to you is because I have an extreme amount of respect for you and you yourself are married, mashAllah. Therefore, if possible, I would kindly appreciate it if you could help me out in this unfortunate predicament. If you would be so kind as to help me find a girl (through your wife or other means), inshAllah (SWT) Allah (SWT) blesses you and rewards you tremendously. Please let me know when you are available to talk, as I would like to discuss this further inshAllah. JazakAllahu Khairan for you time, asalamu alaikum. (Email forwarded to me by my husband)

Ok, you're ready to get married - all you have to do is find the person and you're all set. Unfortunately, like the young man in the email above, many Muslim young adults who desire marriage have a tough time finding a spouse. The social regulation on mixed-gender interactions, coupled with a perceived lack of eligible spouses that fit their marital preferences, have considerably narrowed the number of potential spouses for Muslim young adults. Add to that, Muslim converts, whose families are unable to assist in the search for a Muslim spouse, and we see there is big trouble.

As a result, though open to family help, most American Muslims expect to find their Muslim spouse on their own. One informant joked, *"maybe we'll meet in the grocery store, or take a class together, or something like that."* First, let's explore how individuals find a spouse using their family or either the Muslim community.

FAMILY

> It would be nice to know someone was looking out for me. My parents pressure me into getting married but they aren't doing anything to help me! (Sophomore, South Asian male)

Family. You can't live with them and you can't live without them. With the amount of pressure some families exert on single Muslims, one would expect them to be more active in the search for a spouse. Even the South Asian brothers and sisters whose parents are more accustomed to arranged marriages and who joked about "mobilizing the network of aunties" in their search for a spouse, remarked that the old practice is simply not working anymore. They still can't find a spouse.

Most informants said they do not receive *any* help in their spousal search and they want that to change. Nailah even sees it as the family's responsibility to network and connect in order to find spouses for their children. She says,

> I think people should be encouraged to marry soon after college, and parents should be trying to surround their kids with good potential spouses so they have good pickings. I

> think I am going to be that type of mom. The one who has cute, good brothers and sisters over so my kids will see good potential and just so happen to marry someone I like. I think community is important. The girls in my community whose parents are more networked with other parents got married at good ages, like 22-25 and they married mostly to people in the community... a lot of them married people they've known most of their lives, or for many years. I think parents should be supportive of their kids getting married young. That means money too. It is a trade off for their *deen*.

Nailah's plan to create an environment conducive to finding a spouse for her children is similar to *midang*, a traditional Indonesian courtship practice that involves the courting of an unmarried woman in her natal home (Bennett 2005). Bennett describes *midang* as a way to allow Indonesian youth, the majority of whom are Muslim, to court and yet remain within the boundaries of Islam. During *midang*, the man usually arrives at the woman's home in the early evening and retreats some time before 11pm. Upon his arrival, the young man is greeted by the parents and offered light refreshments. Following a short conversation with parents, the courting couple is either left alone to enjoy each other's company (parents usually stay within earshot). According to Bennett, young men who have become accepted by the family are gradually allowed more access to the more private areas of the home.

Not all arranged marriages are alike.

Midang appears to be a practice enjoyed by both the youth and their parents. Youth are able to enjoy each other's company and parents are able to become familiar with the young man who may become their future son-in-law. Perhaps it can also work in America?

Arranged Marriages

Do arranged marriages exist in America? Yes, they do! In fact many of my informants, both Desi and non-Desi were open to arranged marriages. However, what I discovered is there are several types of arranged marriages. In some arrangements, parents have full authority of choosing the spouse, with or without the consent of the child. However, in other arrangements, the final decision and approval must come from the future spouse.

For example, Fatima assumes that she will have an arranged marriage. She took the time to explain how she envisions the process working for her.

> Well, someone who knows someone who's looking for a wife for their son will approach my mom and say, "*oh you know we know this eligible bachelor.*" This intermediary can be anybody, a relative, a friend of the family, (but) unfortunately if a friend of mine approaches me, it's not the same thing because if my parents don't pre-screen the guy then I guess it's not arranged.
>
> So my parents screen the guys first, get their information, start talking to their families, etc. If my parent okays the guy (that's step one: parent's okay guy, his family okays me), then our parents might arrange a meeting. Maybe I'll meet the guy and he won't be impressed by me. Maybe his family and him will come over and I'll say no. If something happens to click then we go onto stage three (laughing).
>
> We might exchange email addresses or phone numbers and talk to each other, see if we have things in common, goals, etc. Then there's this iffy part…maybe we'll talk for two months, agree we like each other and how we both see the world and get engaged. Or, maybe we'll talk, maybe we'll see each other again, maybe we'll decide this isn't for us. Maybe this will take a month, maybe it will take 5, I don't know ☺. If we get engaged, hopefully (laughing) you'll get married. But even an engagement can be broken off.

I thought, "*Wait a minute, is that how an arranged marriage works? You mean to tell me I had an arranged marriage?*" Though I had never thought of my own marriage as arranged, Fatima's description fit exactly how I met my husband. In fact, when my aunt, who is Christian, told everyone I had an arranged marriage, I almost flipped! I had always viewed an arranged marriage as one without choice. But *I* chose to meet my husband and *I* chose to marry him. Fatima taught me that there are many forms of arranged marriages. She continued with her explanation and said,

> But it's not as Islamic as it should be. I feel an Islamic process should be easier, less confusing… or maybe that's the beauty of it, that no two arranged marriages are the same. Just like no two dating couples have gone through the exact same thing.

"Arranged" had such a negative connotation in the Black Muslim (and American) community. It seems like with most things, when people are uninformed, they tend to dismiss it, or label it as a "bad" cultural practice. We continued and I asked, "*While you are deciding if you like each other, do you also interact in natural settings, e.g. community events or activities, movies, etc?*" Fatima responded,

> Yes and no, those are limited, which is what sucks ☺. You can go out but only with family. But usually that doesn't happen, it's more like you'll get to hang out at each other's houses because no one wants to look bad and send their 23-year-old daughter out with a man she's not even engaged too, even if they take a chaperone with them (hence it's *halal*!).

So here we were again, back at the notion of identity and how decisions are often made in regards to cultural differences more so than Islam. I began to think further about the meaning of identity. Was it true that Muslims are "Muslim First?" My brother brought up the topic later and we discussed how it appears that ethnic and cultural identities surpass often trump Muslim identities. That in reality, Muslim identities only add a few select things to our agenda: prayer, chastity, desire for marriage etc. But that the bulk of our decisions are made in reference to ethnicity and geographical location. For example, yes, Muslims marry, but whom do they marry? After following the Islamic prescript of marriage, it is to their culture (not Islam) that they turn to for a description of a desirable mate, or desirable courtship practice.

THE MASJID

Masjids are the places where Muslims congregate, yet many have not instituted practices or programs aimed at helping single Muslims get married. When I asked one *masjid* leader of a predominately immigrant *masjid* about the *masjid*'s role in helping people find spouses, he responded, *"Well that is not the masjid's ultimate responsibility, it belongs to the family not the masjid."*

It appears that in addition to dropping the ball on programming, many are in effect hindering the process. The strict gender separation of *masjids* has, in the words of Hasan put marriage "far reaching." He states, *"Sis, at my masjid, I never even saw a sister. Now how am I supposed to meet someone in that situation?"*

I only know of one *masjid*, the ADAMS center of Virginia, a pioneer in matrimonial services that runs a regular program for their local community. The Imam and his wife's program, "Companionships", is set up like a group speed dating event where tables of singles rotate and chat with others in their age bracket. To this, Suleiman states,

Sometimes at the Masjid you don't know who is single… the Internet is much easier to find someone

> I think it's really hard to meet good people through your parents or even on your own, just because the community is so small. I applaud all those *imams* who take the time to help out people in their communities.

Muslim young adults want help and assistance from community leaders (but without a negative stigma). Many described ways they thought the Muslim community could assist them in finding a spouse, including holding matrimonial events. Suleiman, the brother who lives in an area with no single women gave a few suggestions.

> I think [*masjids* and the Muslim communities can] start earlier in making the process *halal* (permissible) and

> teaching kids about the right way to do things early and often. There is no shame or shyness in this religion, so teach them well to make the right choices….Also make events to get people to meet or meet their *makhrams* (male guardians) to discuss what they're looking for themselves or their daughters/sisters. Help the singles meet each other and make connections. Know that if you have 70% single men, like we do, that you should plan some trips to communities or reach out and see if sisters want to get married. We need to take the shame and mystery off the process.

Muslims like Zahra, a convert to Islam, who come from non-Muslim families often have to depend on the Muslim community to help them find a Muslim spouse. She suggests the Muslim community,

> Have more social events in the community specifically for single people so they can meet. If folks want to attend them under Islamic standards of having a chaperone that's fine. But there do need to be more events where single folks can interact with each other.

Due to the reduced role of the *masjid*, many are seeking other ways to fulfill half of their religion. In the past decade, we've seen an explosion in the number of Muslim matrimonial companies established with the goal of providing a service to those Muslims who find it difficult to marry. For example, my friend and I organized a singles event in which 35 members of the community came. Likewise, Muslim conferences usually include some sort of matrimonial event. For example, The Islamic Society of North America (ISNA) has organized a matrimonial event for several years. In addition, the National Young Muslim Adult conference quoted by Karim (2005) has also held matrimonial events. However, these are annual events and the need is larger than an annual event can handle.

The masjids need to have more events for singles if they are not going to change the way people find spouses - Malik, 30

CYBERISLAM

If your family and *masjid* are not helping the cause and you think your chances of running into your future spouse at the grocery store are slim, the Internet may be your best matrimonial tool. Sites aimed at single Muslims interested in marriage are becoming more and more popular. Try it for your self, on any random day search for "Muslim marriage," "Single Muslims" or "Muslim Matrimonial" on Google and over 20 websites dedicated to Muslim marriage including MuslimMatch.com and zawaj.com, will appear.

These small niche companies compete with the larger mainstream companies like eHarmony or Match.com. For many like Suleiman, who lives in an area with no access to Muslim women, or Zahra who does not attract Muslim men in person, websites like these offer access to a great number of single Muslims. In addition, the Internet is a site where interactions between men and women cannot be strictly regulated. A brother and sister can talk all night by chat, in the privacy of their homes without worrying about what some other Muslim may think about them.

Also, the distance the computer provides helps many individuals like Nazir who are sometimes uncomfortable talking to someone of the opposite sex in person. I asked one brother why he met his wife online when there were several single sisters at his *masjid*. He responded,

> At the *masjids* you don't know who is single or not – they need some type of singles' programs. The Internet was easier, I could meet a lot of people looking for the same thing. I also didn't have to worry about being rejected to my face.

Before I met Halim, I, too, experimented with finding a spouse online. I posted profiles on www.muslimmatch.com and www.zawaj.com. Though I received some hits, I never felt comfortable talking to someone I did not know. I just felt there was no way I could trust them. In fact, this was one of the major complaints of singles in this study. While the internet is convenient, many people prefer face-to-face personal contact. As one sister said, "there are some weirdos out there."

However, I personally know several great couples who met online. Therefore, I have concluded, it is more about the individual than *how* you meet. By getting family and friends involved, rather than courting in private, one may be able to weed out the "weirdos," both male and female. Families that are helping in the spousal search have also begun to use the internet. The following post is from www.zawaj.com:

> *Write Something about Yourself in Your Own Words*
> She was born and raised in the USA, but is of Syrian descent. Her faith in Islam is strong, even though she is continually trying to improve her faith. She wears *hijab*, prays, and fasts. She is very close to her family, and loves to hang out with friends. She does not smoke, drink, go to clubs, and has never dated.
>
> *Write Something about the Type of Person You are Seeking*
> Someone who like her has never dated, and is trying to improve his faith. A man who is not afraid of a strong-willed woman who speaks her mind and has a successful career. Her greatest pet peeve is dishonesty.

Families typically have very clear ideas about suitable spouses and sometimes do not agree with the selection their child/family member makes. The next two stories highlight the bad and good sides of ethnic endogamy within Muslim communities.

REFLECTIONS

How will you/did you meet your spouse? What do you feel about meeting people randomly, or having an arranged meeting?

10

Reason # 8: Family won't accept Cultural Differences

Imagine meeting the man or woman of your dreams. When you're together, you feel the peace and tranquility Allah described between mates. You are so compatible that everyone around you thinks you two should be married. Reflecting on this gift, you thank Allah for sending such a perfect mate. The one who will help you reach *Jannah* (heaven). Then things start to change... you meet your love's family and they don't accept you. You quickly discover that though Muslims often like to think of themselves as a model community, marriage is one topic that reveals some of the uglier sides of the Muslim community, including discrimination and racism. That is what happened to Tariq, Rahma and Isam. Here are their stories.

Tariq – A Man Who May Never Marry

At a time when most kids are worrying about fitting in and what to wear to school the next day, Tariq a high school freshman, was worried about his soul. A mixed African-American, with a Catholic mother and

Baptist father, Tariq has always known and appreciated diversity, *"I saw the beauty and meanings of both the Catholic and Baptist teachings."* When Tariq witnessed firsthand the effects of alcohol on his peers, he began to search for his own religious path. Later in the 11th grade, Tariq officially embraced Islam as a shi'a Muslim and has not looked back since.

To his surprise, Tariq soon discovered that the community he embraced was less of a cultural utopia and more of an intra-racial group. He says,

> When we first become Muslims, we think that South Asians are good Muslims, but you find out that they are like everybody else. There are good Muslims, there are bad Muslims. You take a while to realize that they don't know more than you. Being Muslim is not (always) their primary identity; they're often more Arab or South Asian.

Tariq, a black man of mixed heritage, often felt isolated from the predominately South Asian and Arab believers who tried to "recreate back home." He often found himself visiting the predominately African-American Sunni community, which was more "open, tolerant and accepting." As a shi'a, Tariq was unique and did not fit the normal Black Sunni conversion experience (the overwhelming majority of African-American Muslims are Sunni).

It was on campus, that Tariq found the openness he longed for. Though still one of the few Blacks in the Muslim organizations (many African-American Muslims chose to join the Black Student Union over the MSA, a "cultural association,") Tariq found that his new fellow Muslim peers, mostly second generation Muslims, did not hold the same views of their immigrant parents. They were more "multicultural" and very much a part of the diverse, socially active campus. He says, *"Having engagement with other friends adds so much flavor to my life."* That 'flavor' included a relationship with a beautiful young *muslima.*

Shazia was active in the community, and like Tariq, willing to take a stand on important issues and put herself on the line for what she believed. In many ways, she and Tariq were the perfect couple. However, Shazia was South Asian and her parents were not fond of their daughter's choice of suitors. Tariq remembers them telling her things like, *"He's tricked you, he's just saying sweet things to you."* It was if Shazia's parents treated their relationship like they "were in middle school."

After nearly seven years together, Shazia called off their relationship. She could no longer handle the stress and it became apparent that her parents, who desired a South Asian groom from a Muslim family, would never accept Tariq. He continues, *"not only was their racism involved, but there was social elitism. There was this idea that anyone who did not come from a Muslim family would cause trouble."* Tariq was devastated. The woman he loved and wanted to marry had chosen to preserve ties with her family over marrying him. After long hours of reflection and prayers for guidance (*istikhara*), Tariq took a personal vow never to marry anyone else. He had prayed for Allah to show him the way. *"I told her parents if I can not marry Shazia, then I will not marry at all,"* recounted Tariq. Though he wishes it had been his significant other Shazia who had the courage to make the vow, (he still refers to her as his significant other), he understands the importance of family. It has been two years and Shazia has now accepted to marry a South Asian man. We discussed his plans now that Shazia's imminent marriage is here. Interspersed with talk about being with Shazia in *Jannah* (heaven), Tariq states his vow to never marry another woman is final. He made a symbolic contract with Allah that he does not plan to break.

Being Muslim is not always the primary identity; it's often more South Asian or Arab

However, there is a twist. I was itching to understand if Tariq's vow of 'No Marriage' also extends to "No Sex." Tariq explained that within Shi'a Islam there exists *muta'a* or temporary marriage. In the marriage contract, couples specify the date upon which the marriage shall end. The practice is highly controversial, one that Sunni Muslims (roughly 85% of the Muslim population) and most shi'a believe was outlawed during the Prophet's time (Haeri 1989). While Tariq is not sure he will take advantage of *muta'a* which could legalize sexual relationships for as short as a few minutes to several years, he plans to leave the option open if he is desperately in need.

Tariq now speaks publically about his vow to never marry and about the marital racism and social elitism he has endured. He and Shazia are still friends and Tariq supported her in her husband selection. He vows to change the system by "coming out of the closet," drawing an analogy to the similarities between the stigma placed on those who never marry and to those who are gay. Both, deemed unacceptable behaviors in the Muslim community.

RAHMA AND ISAM – A STORY OF LOVE ON HOLD

Imagine not being able to marry the one you love – all because you have a different family background

"*Rahma and Isam are officially engaged!*" Though they never publicized their relationship, most in their Detroit *masjid* and university suspected they were a couple. From the first time I saw Rahma, a tall Palestinian-American and Isam, a tall Indian-American, I too had a hunch they were romantically involved or at least had a mutual crush. And the more I ran into them in Detroit, the more obvious it became. For example, at events, Isam would be sure to purchase the 100% juice Rahma desired, and Rahma's stories always included Isam. Though I never asked directly (I didn't feel it was my business), I felt stifled by their secrecy. Should I acknowledge the relationship or play along with the game?

When I began to do my research, it became even more awkward. I had approached nearly every single Muslim I knew, including Rahma. While I was grateful that she agreed to an interview, I soon abandoned the idea. I could feel that she was not very comfortable with the idea and honestly neither was I. I did not want to put her in position to lie and I knew she would not/could not tell her story in full. Accordingly, I simply made myself unavailable. When the interview came up a month later, I decided to change the interview's focus from personal experiences, to safer questions like *masjid* relations or gender separation.

I sent her a text message with the new topic, but ironically, just a few hours later the news of their engagement broke. Finally! I was so excited for them but I admit I felt a selfish sense of relief. Now I could talk to her without having to let on that I suspected she was in a relationship. In response to my text message, Rahma called back and for the first time in 3 years, she and I had a real conversation. Though I did not audio tape our spontaneous talk, I choose to represent it here in dialogue format.

Z: Congratulations! I heard the news!

R: Thanks! So you heard?

Z: Yeah, Halim called me. I am SOOO excited for you! This is beautiful. Alhamdulillah!

R: [Laughing] Yeah, Alhamdulillah. I so wanted to tell you yesterday (we were at a wedding together the day before) but I couldn't.

Z: I know. I mean everyone knew that you two would eventually get engaged, it was just a matter of when. I mean why were you guys so dang ole secretive?

R: I know it was so hard, not being able to tell anyone. I mean Isam and I have loved each other for the past 4 years but we couldn't tell. You know how Muslims are, our reputations would have been ruined! But we also had to wait for our parents to agree and that took some time.

Z: I understand, but girl you can't worry about those people! They're gonna talk anyway.

R: I know. I remember when you asked me for an interview, I really wanted to tell you but I couldn't.

Z: Yeah, I figured so. That's partially why I didn't pursue it. Well anyway, I'm so excited for you! I feel so much better because now I can talk to you for real! [laughing]

R: What do you mean?

Z: [Laughing] Well, I always felt somewhat weird around you. I was always watching my words, trying not to let on that I viewed you and Isam as a couple. I mean it was just so awkward…I really tried to avoid you!

> **R:** [laughing], you could have just asked me (laughing). Aminah and Didi did. They came up and asked me if I liked somebody in the MSA. I admitted yes... go on facebook and see who is in all of my pictures! They came back like "Isam!?"
>
> **Z:** (laughing) Well it seemed like a secret, plus, it's really not any of my business anyway! I mean we don't hang out on a regular basis and we're not as close as you, Aminah and Didi so I shouldn't ask you about your personal business. I'm just glad everything is out now so that we can just be free!
>
> **R:** Me too! Now we can hang out, go to the movies, do double dates and stuff!

As we talked, I thought about how difficult this whole process must have been for Rahma and Isam - having to put their love on hold simply because of cultural differences. I told Rahma I definitely appreciated her sharing her story – I thought it might be useful for others going through the same situation.

> **R:** I know, I think the beauty of Isam and my relationship is that we will be able to build the *ummah* (Muslim community). I mean we're from two different backgrounds, maybe it will help.

So Rahma was concerned about their reputations? And their families did not agree? This was getting interesting! Now that she could explain, Rahma and I set a date for when I returned to Detroit and for the first time, I was not hesitant about calling her back. When we met we talked about secrets, cultural differences, parents and how the past four years have been pure hell for them both. When walking on Oakland University's campus, they were always looking over their shoulder to see who is there. How had it all started? Rahma took me back to the beginning,

> I had just started to be more religious and I had decided I was not going to have a non-Muslim boyfriend again. I

> was a freshman and I went to my first MSA meeting. Honestly, I think I also wanted to meet a Muslim guy too. So I saw Isam and I really liked him, but all the girls liked him. He was the only American (smiling)! But Isam and I became friends. We talked about stuff and I really started to like him! Only my non-Muslim friends knew. Then one day a mutual (Muslim) and I were out shopping. I can remember it so vividly. We were looking at some clothes and she asked me if I ever thought about Isam. I flipped out and went into this long explanation, 'Noooo! I don't like him…. how could I like him? Ugh, he's like my brother!' My friend was like 'aww man Rahma, this is terrible because he is so in love with you!' Man I got scared because I realized I might mess this thing up for good. So I confessed that I really liked him too but that I wanted to tell him myself. So the next day we (Isam and I) talked and I punked out (laughing), I was too shy. But then the next day he called and he just asked me point blank. I said yes and the rest is history!

For the next four years, Rahma and Isam cultivated their relationship through phone calls and Muslim events. Isam said, "I would have married her from the first time we talked." Rahma continued, "Our parent's didn't agree." Due to cultural differences and their student status, neither set of parents agreed to the marriage or courtship. Both parents wanted their children to marry someone of the same ethnicity (Palestinian and Indian). The fact Isam was a "broke college student" did not help the case. Rahma and Isam were devastated. When I asked if they ever thought of getting married without their parents' blessing Isam replied, "Well I knew my mom wouldn't come." At my surprised face, he explained, "I remember one day when I was talking to my mom. I mentioned that there was a girl…that's all I said. I didn't even say Rahma (laughing) and my mom didn't talk to me for 3 months!" After four years of negotiations with their

We hope our inter-racial marriage will make a difference in the community - Rahma and Isam

parents, Rahma and Isam finally won their blessing and they both sigh with, "Alhamdulillah (All praises due to God) it's over." But is it over?

On the Sunday prior to our interview, the new couple held an engagement party with forty members of their family and closest friends. It was a beautiful occasion "filled with blessing" but it also foreshadowed a few hurdles their new combined family face. The party was split, not only by gender (as is customary) but by race with the Indian and Palestinian women on different sides of the room. However, the men were more intermingled. Isam explained,

> I think that has more to do than just with cultural differences. I mean these are all professional men with careers. They are used to being outside of their comfort zone and intermingling with people. The women who were there don't work, so they are not used to that. I mean my mom has a job but it is not a career. [...] But I was mad they (my family) were speaking Urdu.

Language barriers are often one of the main reasons family members site the necessity to marry within. Without communication and a conscious effort to be close, language can be a natural divider. Wedding traditions are another divider. Isam described how the party would have been different with an Indian fiancé.

> They would have had these huge wooden trays filled with gifts for Rahma and covered with a velvet heavily embroidered cloth. The women of my family would each present Rahma with a small gift and then her side would do the same thing for me. That's why I think my mom still doesn't look at this as the engagement party. She said it was more like (Urdu term that translated as "talk confirmed"). I think she still wants to do another engagement party later.

Traditionally Indian engagement parties are extremely expensive, something Isam and his parents were unable to afford. Both he and Rahma are more than satisfied with their small intimate gathering. The engagement party was just one experience but the wedding will be another and reveals just how much negotiation will be needed to please both families. In a traditional Indian wedding, the bride wears a red dress and adopts a very subdued demeanor (not a lot of smiling or talking, etc). But Rahma's Palestinian mother prefers a white wedding dress. Rahma is caught in the middle. They may have found a solution.

> Well for my family the signing of the *kitab* (Islamic marriage contract) is the most important so for that she'll wear the red. And for her family, the *Walima* (celebration party) is the most important, so there she'll wear white. *InshaAllah* everyone will be happy (Isam)

Obviously, family is very important to both Rahma and Islam and they have gone through a lot of trouble to appease their families' traditions and desires. Not only did they wait four years to be engaged, they are also making compromises to their wedding ceremony. They want to get married as soon as possible, the couple is now negotiating the complicated terms of their future marriage, there is a possibility of conducting an Islamic marriage contract prior to the licensed marriage.

Isam explains that in Indian culture, the couple would probably be married now. At the 'engagement ceremony,' Rahma and Isam would have signed an Islamic marriage contract stating the stipulations (including dowry) of their marriage. They would then be married Islamically, but would not move in together until after the big *walima* (wedding party and ceremony with the state marriage license). In this scenario (according to Indian Muslim culture but not Islamic law), Isam would be absolved of his financial agreement until the walima at which time the marriage would be consummated. And that's where the problem lies.

In Rahma's culture, both the Islamic marriage and legal marriage occur on the same day. Her parents are not comfortable with Isam's scenario in which the couple is Islamically married but waiting to consummate, "accidents could happen." For Rahma and Isam to consummate their relationship, not only must they be married, Isam must also take full financial responsibility for her. It seems that sex is on everyone's mind except Rahma and Isam. Isam explained, *"I don't think our parents understand. It was a fear of God that kept us from haram (sin) during these four years, so it will be the fear of God that keeps us from wrong now too."*

Now that their families have agreed, there is just one last hurdle to jump, Isam's lack of financial resources. At the time of our interview, Isam was a full time graduate student with graduate student income, "less than a quarter of what a plumber makes and I have six years of higher education!" With the responsibility to provide for his wife in mind, Isam has agreed to follow his dad's decision and wait to get married until he is financially able to support Rahma. Isam's mother has always had to work and he does not want the same for Rahma. *"I want her (Rahma) to be able to stay home if she wants to, at least when we have kids ... I don't expect for us to make a whole bunch of money but I do want to be able to provide for our necessities and maybe a few of the wants."*

Isam is now saving money. In the meantime, they are simply ecstatic. Isam replied, "*Alhamdulillah, we can finally walk on campus without having to look over our shoulder!*" They both laugh. With their formal engagement, Isam and Rahma have made their intentions publically known. Their parents still have parameters on what they can and cannot do (e.g. Rahma still hasn't been given permission to drive to Baltimore with Isam alone), but they now have much more freedom.

EXOGAMY - A SHIFT IN MARITAL TRADITIONS

Popular discourse and research (Grewal 2008) indicate that young Muslims are increasingly more open to marriages and relationships outside of their race. However, as Tariq learned, though Muslims often exalt the beauty of a global *ummah* where, "*an Arab has no superiority over a non-Arab nor a non-Arab has any superiority over an Arab; also a white has no superiority over black nor a black has any superiority over white except by piety and good action*" (excerpt from Prophet Muhammad's farewell sermon), when it pertains to marrying outside of one's racial/ethnic background, the true "imagined" nature of this community is revealed.

Young Muslims who reject the endogamous marriage practices of their parents' cultures often incur huge obstacles. Parents often threaten to disown their child or not offer financial support for the wedding ceremony. In Chapter 2, I highlighted Grewal's study of the intra-racial color preferences of second-generation Muslim immigrants and their parents (2008). Several informants and their families coveted whiteness as the ideal sign of beauty and marriageablity. However, many in the second-generation refer to the Quran to "Islamify" their actions in the hopes that faced with Islamic evidence, their parents will have no choice but to agree to an inter-racial marriage.

Though a struggle, some single Muslims have successfully negotiated the reluctant approval of their families. Rahma and Isam's experience highlights a number of both beautiful and troubling parts of Muslim American singlehood. Their struggle to do something Islamic (get married), has been met with severe opposition and complications from the start, again revealing that when it comes to marriage, parents and individuals are often much more attached to their cultural identities than their religious identities. On the beautiful side, the next generation of Muslims is pushing for a new agenda, a new way of business. Rahma and Isam could have given up their quest for marriage but they chose to fight back, supported by the knowledge that their behavior was perfectly legal in the eyes of their Lord. Their relationship and future marriage is one of opposition to the status-quo of Muslim ethnic endogamy, and perhaps their experience may change the tradition. At least for now, they take comfort knowing the story will be different for their future children.

PART II SUMMARY

As religious minorities in a pluralistic society, single American Muslims are influenced by a multitude of cultural systems including religion, personal beliefs, popular culture, family, and ethnicity. This chapter highlighted some of the ways these systems produce ambivalence and challenges for Muslim singles negotiating singlehood, religion and desires. The stories of Nadirah, Ali and Tahira highlight the choice to be Muslim and how some young Muslims live dual lives - a Muslim life inside of the *masjid*, and a "normal" student life outside of the *masjid* and Muslim spaces. Many young Muslims are curious about life outside of Islam and choose college, a time away from parents, to fulfill their curiosity. They often feel torn between an Islamic prohibition on premarital sex and physically intimate behaviors, and the normative sexual behaviors of their peers. While some Muslims remain within Islamic boundaries, many others step outside those boundaries. As the literature suggests, the Muslims who strongly identified with Islamic teachings tend to experiment less with drugs, sex and physical intimacy than those whose Islamic identification is less salient (Freitas 2008).

Secondly, after college, family and community members begin to pressure Muslims to marry as soon as possible. While most Muslim young adults are not opposed to getting married, they feel the culture of the Muslim communities does not foster marriage. For one thing, interactions between Muslims of the opposite sex are rare, and single individuals often have no way of identifying each other. Further, many Muslims who grew up in strictly gendered Islamic spaces are uncomfortable around Muslims of the opposite sex, and couldn't imagine approaching someone Muslim for marriage. However, experiences in non-gendered settings like college and office environments, allow for cross-gender interaction facilitating much more conversation amongst non-Muslims. For example, Tahira states, many people are more comfortable with "John at work than Muhammad at the *masjid*."

As a result, the question is not one of *whether* to get married, but of *who* to marry and finding a spouse has proven difficult. American Muslims overwhelmingly expect a "love marriage," one in which they are familiar with their future spouse prior to actual marriage. Unfortunately, cross-gender interactions are usually socially unacceptable. Lastly, tensions often arise between young adults who are open to marrying outside of their ethnic background and their parents who do not agree to these inter-ethnic marriages. Though their children are within the boundaries of Islamic behaviors, these examples highlight how ethnic identities sometimes trump religious identities.

PART III

Action Steps and Conclusions

11

Easing the Path Of Singlehood

Given the experiences of single Muslim young adults, what course of action should be taken by the community as a whole? Throughout this study, several informants and members of the community inquired about my recommendations to correct some of what I mentioned in this book. I would often ask the same questions of them. Based on both of our responses, the suggestions included in this chapter center on addressing three underlying issues: 1) Construction of American Muslim hybrid identities, 2) lack of dialogue in the community around singlehood, and 3) ways to redefine singlehood.

Healthy American Muslim Hybrid Identities

Living in a pluralistic society affords individuals the opportunity to test various "truths." As such, many young Muslims are curious about other lifestyles and often delay becoming "full" Muslims until they have had the opportunity to experience the other side. Those curious moments are often kept secret from the Muslim community and many Muslims lead double lives. At the *Masjid*, they perform the "good Muslim" identity, and in non-Muslim spaces, they perform the "regular American" identity. They are not able to completely hybridize and blend their realities.

This dual life of secrecy can take its toll, but it also indicates that for many young Muslims, society, not God is most influential to their behaviors. The fear of earning a bad reputation or bringing shame to parents is a major deciding factor for many youth. This is interesting because Muslims hold the view that Allah (God) is all-knowing, all-encompassing. One would assume this to mean that a Muslim is always concerned about their actions in relation to their Lord, rather than to their parents or other community members.

We need institutions that support a Muslim way of life

We have seen that many Muslims are looking for ways to hybridize American Islam and reduce the stress that comes from living in an ambivalent third space. In a religiously pluralistic society, it is important to recognize the efforts of community leaders to "stake out a distinctive *local* space for expressions of religious life, where people make sense of themselves as having a collective identity" (Moore 2007:116). Several people suggest that the way to do this is to provide a social network which values being Muslim.

For example, at a fundraising dinner for MANA, a Muslim organization founded to address the social ails facing indigenous Muslims, two prominent Blackamerican Muslims, Dr. Sherman Jackson and Imam Siraj Wahaj, gave dynamic talks on identity, youth, networking and improving the social status of American Muslims. Dr. Jackson suggested that the community provide support spaces for Muslims. Spaces that affirm "Muslim" ways of life as the connection between a young person and God and Islam is weakened when their surroundings do not support the same values.

Likewise, Eboo Patel, a scholar and founder of a Chicago based organization working to remove religious prejudice amongst youth, wrote a telling short paper on nurturing a modern Muslim identity. Though Patel is arguing within the framework of developing "moderate" Muslims, his point that individuals construct a Muslim identity based on what religious education is available to them, is relevant for any aspect of Muslim identities. Until Muslims have mainstream institutions - schools and universities, political organizations, publishing houses, television and radio programs, magazines, youth organizations and women's groups - that influence young people in a "Muslim" way, Muslim youth will continue to be pulled away from Islam. Patel illustrates his point with a great food analogy of a vegetarian in Chicago:

> Many of my students come from small towns around the Midwest. Several became vegetarians when they moved to Chicago. When they return home, they find it difficult to refrain from eating meat. The reason is simple: In Chicago, the institutions of vegetarianism abound. There are several excellent vegetarian restaurants, many grocery stores have large sections of vegetarian items, vegetarian cookbooks are readily available in bookstores and communities of vegetarians are not hard to find. Such institutions are a rarity in Rantool and Kankakee, and therefore a vegetarian identity is difficult to maintain in those areas (Patel 2003:2).

This simple example is clearly very powerful in revealing the importance of supportive institutions. Many young adults explore life outside of Islam purely out of curiosity. What they see outside of Islam seems much more exciting than the "lectures we attend at the *Masjid.*" By providing healthy Muslim alternatives to the regular "clubbing, drinking and sexing," the temptations may lessen.

OPEN DIALOGUE AND REMOVING THE STIGMA

When American Muslim identities are created, the diversity within must then be supported through open dialogue. Muslims often complain that the Muslim community is too judgmental, and that if and when an individual holds a different interpretation from the majority, they are made to feel less "Muslim" and labeled a "cultural" Muslim. This study has shown that there is no one "Muslim" way and subsequently, no singular American Muslim identity. As such, the institutions created must be open to dialogue and dissenting views. Moore argues, "variations in ideology, theology, and degree of religiosity are highly contingent on pressures toward conformity exerted upon individuals in one instance by an external authority – the *ummah* – and in another by the internal dynamics of the homeland" (Moore 2007: 116-117).

Muslim communities want members who conform to their modes of thinking and behaving, and Muslim singles are forced to live those aspects of their lives that differ from the hegemonic ideals in secret. Because of the taboo on gender interactions and behaviors that contradict perceived Muslim ideals, many Muslim young adults conduct their singlehood in privacy, away from the Muslim public's judging eyes. As a result, these young adults often feel marginalized and pushed away from the Muslim communities in which they live.

By creating spaces for open dialogue within the Muslim community, single Muslims may not only feel more connected to the community, they may be more comfortable finding a spouse on their own terms (whether it be arranged or otherwise) which would then provide the basis of strong families for the community to build upon. For example, when I asked Fatima how she thought Muslim singlehood could improve, she suggested a new way of thinking, specifically in reference to courtship and Pakistani-American arranged marriages.

> I think people need to open up a little and realize that two people can get to know each other respectfully without resorting to anything inappropriate (although hormones are pesky little things and I wouldn't be surprised if more people have slipped up than not LOL). But there should be more acceptance with families about people meeting each other. There's a stigma in our culture to anything "not arranged." But everyone does it, my cousin that lives with us totally picked out his wife, she was an old friend from Qatar or something. They started chatting then talking, etc. But there's no blame on him, maybe because he's a guy? Or maybe because he didn't make it a big deal?

Gender differences must also be addressed. Parents who give men more leeway with social activities are seen as setting a double standard. If premarital sex is prohibited for men and women, why wouldn't both sexes have the same level of constraints? After all, a woman cannot impregnate herself (naturally). Fatima continues,

> And other times people meet and go out of their way to pretend it was arranged which is silly. Be open about - it will help people be more accepting. This might not make sense but what I'm really saying is A) can we stop having double standards for men and women? B) be honest, if you meet someone don't lie and act like it's a shameful thing because you're making it more stigmatized you know, and C) maybe people (elders) will eventually be a little bit more open and trusting. And yes this applies to the parents of ABCDs (American Born Confused Desis) here.

Pretending for the benefit of the community implies a lack of connection and faith in God. I am not saying one should blast wrongdoings, but I am talking about those activities that are within the bounds of Islam but simply seen as taboo. It also highlights the human tendency to conform to society. As a result of both, many activities are indeed cultural rather than religious in nature. The stigmas community members can place on individuals who go against the status-quo are part of what can make life on earth a living hell. In order for people to be honest, they must first have a safe place to land and the Muslim community must provide that place. For example, as a convert with no Muslim family, Zahra sees the *masjid* as the only place she would be able to meet a Muslim spouse. She wants the elders to facilitate conversations between the sexes, or at a minimum "not flip out."

> Singlehood is hard, especially when you are trying to be the "ideal" Muslim. And brothers and sisters and elders in the *Ummah* need to understand that. I'm not making any excuses, but ideal is different from reality, and hopefully we can collectively come together to try to make life for single Muslims a little easier rather than just putting our heads in the sand to the issue. I mean maybe they could

> not flip out when they see two unmarried persons of the opposite gender talking out in the open to each other after *Jumah.* I am speaking from a younger person's perspective. I use that example because an elder, or a Muslim with a more conservative understanding of the *deen*, may actually scare these young folks into thinking what they are doing is wrong, and then they will sneak off to talk to each other. And that won't help anything...so I guess in a nutshell, find a happy medium to the gender separation issue.

As I indicated, many Muslim young adults are more comfortable with non-Muslims of the opposite sex than with other Muslims. Not only does this negatively affect the strength of our Muslim communities, it also reduces the number of perceived potential spouses. I often heard such statements as, "I don't know any Muslim sisters well enough to marry them" or "I don't even know who is single at my *masjid*." Open dialogue could assist young Muslims to feel more comfortable with Muslim members of the opposite sex. As well as give them the room to question those things they do not understand and in the process strengthen their personal connection to God.

I mean come on, can we at least talk about these issues out in the open? - Lisa

A New Breed of Muslim Organizations – Seven Shades

Muslim organizations like MAS Youth, MYNA, Seven Shades and others are providing additional spaces for community dialogue. For example, in March 2008, 35 youth and young adults ranging in age from 12-36 came together to participate in the first Seven Shades retreat. Nestled in a large log cabin with a gorgeous view of Lake Michigan just a few feet away, the setting proved useful to accomplish the weekend's goals: to provide a safe space for young Muslims from a variety of backgrounds to discuss their true feelings about Islam, family, *masjid* relations, economics, and of course, gender.

Following registration and dinner, my husband Halim, the group's president, greeted us and laid the ground rules: no judging and no disrespecting of anyone's point of view. "*This weekend is a chance to talk and air some things out… we're going to kick things off with our first session on gender relations."* Participants all looked around and exchanged glances conveying the message "wow, what a topic to start off the retreat!" Using a sliding wall, one of the brothers divided the room, brothers on one side and sisters on the other. After 45 minutes, the brothers and sisters were to come back together and share out in a larger group.

People should be able to marry at young ages – it will make the whole process easier - Nadia

In the sisters' section, we discussed several topics including gender separation of the *masjids*, Muslim brothers who marry non-Muslim sisters, matters of dress and a seemingly shortage of available spouses. A few married sisters mentioned the need for premarital counseling. As a group, we came up with questions to pose to the brothers. Our questions included "*what do you look for in a wife,*" "*what do you feel when you see a Muslim sister talking to men (like on campus)*" and "*why do you talk to non-Muslim sisters when there are so many Muslim sisters available?*" Some of the brothers' questions were, "*How do we approach a sister?*" And "*How do we tell the difference between the sisters who are like "Get away from me I'm Muslim" and those who would be receptive?*"

The sisters responded that they would like to be approached respectfully, not "*Yo baby can I get your number.*" Or if the brothers are not sure, they could approach a family member or friend and go through an intermediary. That led to the next question from the sisters, "*Why do you all talk to non-Muslim girls at school but don't talk to us?*" The brothers responded that it's easier (no intermediary) and they already know where they stand with non-Muslim women. Due to shifting levels of appropriateness, many Muslims, men and women alike stick with what is safe and comfortable – conversations with non-Muslims.

Like the workshop Karim (2005) documented, the retreat illustrated the huge need for dialogue without judgment. The brothers and sisters clearly had several questions for each other and this provided them with a space to answer those questions in an open manner. In fact, for many of this study's informants, being interviewed was the first time they were able to discuss their true feelings on their own terms without fear of negative judgment. As a result, many interviewees appreciated and enjoyed the interview process itself.

MARRIAGE IN STAGES: NIKAH NOW, SEX AND MARRIAGE LATER.

It appears there is a growing trend of Muslim couples to consider conducting their marriages in stages. The word *nikah* means marriage in Arabic, it signifies the formal Islamic marriage contract that binds two individuals. Colloquially, in America the term *nikah* may or may not refer to the marriage license filed with the state, nor does it always refer to the big *walima* (marriage party/reception). Some Muslims perform all three actions at once, an Islamic marriage contract, a legally binding marriage with the state, and have a wedding reception announcing the wedding to the community. However, others spread the process over a certain length of time.

There are varieties of ways the marriage can occur. Here I provide two versions. Both Aliyah and Mirza see "staged" marriages as a good solution to many of issues single Muslim young adults face. Aliyah's version is based on her brother's recent marriage.

> For my brother and sister in law, they got engaged for a few months but they are both pretty strict. They kept emailing each other, not really talking face to face unless someone else was with them. No touching and stuff. She was my cousin's Quran teacher and they were both looking so my aunt hooked them up. Then they got their nikah in the *masjid*. We had a party in the gym, then later we came over to her house and she had her hair all done and my dad and my brother were allowed to come in and they danced to some *nasheed* (form of Islamic Music). So now they are basically what non Muslims would call dating, hanging out with each other, getting to know each other, going out to dinner, movies, holding hands.

At this stage of the "marriage", the couple can be married Islamically, but not necessarily legally. Under Islamic law they are able to consummate their marriage. In this case, Aliyah's brother and his wife were married both Islamically *and* legally, but physical intimacy was limited to holding hands and hugging until the big formal wedding. Aliyah says,

"I guess the nikah thing is just a way for them to get to know each other very well within the limits of Islam."

Aliyah describes this scenario as an exception to the rule because of her family's cultural diversity. Her father is White, her mother is *Desi* and her sister-in-law is Arab. According to Aliyah, "*the traditional Desi way is that you get engaged, then you get nikahed and live with the guy, no in between part. But I guess it's all flexible.*" In regards to financial responsibility, Aliyah responded, "*culturally your parents are responsible, but religiously it's the other way around.*" Aliyah believes when she gets married, her parents (or her husband's parents) would be responsible for the couple for a time being. Several Muslim young adults including Mirza believe this is a solution to the struggle for marriage, parents should encourage young marriages and help support them until they can fully support themselves. Here is his version of a *nikah*.

> A lot of young Muslim couples today are getting married without moving in with each other and so as long as the marriage is not consummated, there is no financial burden on the brother. It's sort like what I refer to as 'Islamic dating' (laughing). (The man is only responsible after consummating). I think it's a very viable way for young Muslims who are in college for example to get married. You can get married Islamically and legally. You can go to the movies, get ice cream haha. I wouldn't mind that honestly because sometimes I just feel that I need a female companion, I mean besides the carnal desires that we all have.

Later I asked Mirza to explain why in his version, the couple does not consummate following the marriage.

> Because the brother is not financially able to support his wife...i.e. he is not in a position for her to live with him. It's sort of like having a *halal* (permissible) girlfriend lol … I mean that's one of the fundamental obligations of the man…to be the breadwinner -it's not an optional thing. But here's the thing, if your parents, for example are willing to pay for your apartment and other living costs for you, then there's no problem, she can live with you. But I

for one, would feel embarrassed to put my parents in such a position.

Waiting until later to consummate the marriage also provides the opportunity for the couple to get to know each other. If they should happen to divorce, they could maintain their virginity until their permanent marriage. In Mirza's example, the reasoning for this type of "marriage in stages" rest on finances. It allows a young man to marry without the full financial responsibilities and allows a young woman to marry without having to wait until she or her husband have a bachelor's degree. In my opinion, this type of marriage ONLY works with both emotional and financial support from one's family and community. Couples on their own, encountering inevitable hardships may be more likely to divorce.

"It takes a village to support healthy American Muslim marriages." American Muslims face a number of challenges in both negotiating religious identities in America as well as finding a suitable spouse. Studies like this, which aim to highlight the situation as well as provide possible solutions, may help improve the lives of a great number of single Muslims by raising awareness. Whether the implemented solution is marriage in stages as Aliyah and Mirza suggest, or simply family members keeping a look out for a potential spouse, the community and family will be integral to the success of the chosen initiatives.

But one thing is clear, the stigma on being single and desiring to be married must be removed. Though the Muslim community often states they want people to be married, unmarried Muslims are not receiving the support they need to achieve that. Single Muslims should be able to express their desires without fear of being seen as "on the prowl" or for sisters as being too aggressive and forward.

12

Conclusions: Living Muslim Singlehood In The Third Space

What the future holds for the American Muslim community is strongly based on the experiences of today's youth and young adults. Muslims' identities are complicated and multifaceted, yet interestingly this research shows that most American Muslims across ethnic and racial boundaries are facing common issues with singlehood. It is the negotiation of competing cultural wombs coupled with the natural human desire to maintain a sense of inner peace and harmony (as well as social acceptance), that pushes single Muslims into the *third space* (Bhabha 1994). Here, in this liminal identity space, young Muslims internalize and hybridize their influences and enact their singlehood accordingly. Naturally, this process is fluid and by extension, the singlehood of Muslim young adults is a historicized contextual process. With this in mind, I have attempted to highlight the diversity of how Muslims negotiate their Muslim singlehood; specifically how three cultural wombs; Islam, America, and their family/ethnic backgrounds influence single Muslims' decisions and emotions.

All of these various, competing ideologies force Muslims to actively and consciously define their brand of Islam, their morality and their singlehood. Hence, this book used a critical lens to highlight the difficulties of American Muslim singlehood. For example, with religion, basic Islamic tenets of a belief in God, the Prophethood of Muhammad, and the afterlife greatly affect the worldviews of single

Muslims and play a huge role in deciding whether to act on sexual desires. Young Muslims who are Muslim in speech, but not heart, naturally feel freer to explore life outside of Islamic boundaries. And as they grow older, how they choose to practice and enact a Muslim identity is their decision alone.

While single Muslims agree that singlehood should be temporary, many feel as if they have no prospects for ending it, they are simply putting their faith in God that their spouse will someday arrive. Though there are obviously both male and female singles that are looking to be married, there appears to be no intermediary, no process by which they meet. This uncertainty adds an additional layer of stress because there is no light at the end of the tunnel. In addition, the gender segregation practiced at many *masjids* is not helping the situation.

Many of the issues single Muslims face, are felt by all American Muslims. Stronger communities centered around the masjid and other institutions will be a benefit for the community as a whole.

The *Masjid* is the center of the Muslim community, the major place where Muslims congregate in a non-Muslim society. Accordingly, one would assume that it affords the most opportunity to meet someone of the opposite sex. Yet it is here where interaction and even conversations between the opposite sexes are taboo and cause for community judgment. The Muslims who describe feeling "weird" around Muslims of the opposite sex ask, *"How can I find a spouse if I can't even see them!"*

When I talked to one Detroit Imam about organizing singles events, he suggested that if the Muslim community was organized the way it should be, singles events would be unnecessary. Two Muslims would be able to get to know each other in a Muslim environment without the pressure of making a quick decision of whether to pursue marriage or not. He argued that being able to observe a person's mannerisms, the events they attend, and the activities they volunteer for, would be the best pre-marital situation.

What the Imam describes is creating a culture of marriage. Not one in which individuals are pressured to marry, but one in which individuals are cultivated and prepared for marriage in an Islamic environment. In that environment, expressing interest in someone would not be cause for stress, but instead a normal part of getting married. With the whole community committed to fashioning an atmosphere that supports single individuals (whether by providing opportunities to create an active social life or by facilitating ways for them to meet), there may be a flicker of hope for young Muslims trying to end singlehood.

This type of environment may also strengthen the Muslim community as a whole. By fostering a community of dialogue, individuals, both brothers and sisters will be more likely to work together to further the mission of the Muslim communities. Organizations must have open and clear lines of communication to succeed. While men have traditionally run *Masjids* and Islamic organizations, women are becoming a stronger force in American Islam. I shall cite just one recent example. In 2006, Dr. Ingrid Mattison, a Muslim woman, became the president of the Islamic Society of North America, one of the largest Muslim advocacy organizations in America. In this pivotal role, imagine if she or those she works with were unable to work through some of the ambivalence informants of this study articulated around interactions with Muslims of the opposite sex. Or if strict gender separation governed the office. The organization would certainly fail.

DOES THE THIRD SPACE END?

I have argued that the third space for many Muslim singles is filled with ambivalence. But is it indeed liminal? And is it temporary? Will ending singlehood effectively move young Muslims out of the third space and into a more cemented, less negotiated way of life? In Bhabha's view, third spaces are "discursive sites or conditions that ensure that the meaning and symbols of culture have no primordial unity or fixity; that even the same signs can be appropriated, translated, and rehistoricized anew" (Bhabha 1994:37). That is, the third space insures that Muslim culture is not static. That the conditions that created the third space of Muslim singlehood will shift and bring to existence new conditions which shall again lead to ambiguity and necessitate hybridity. Thus, the social contexts in which American Muslims live will undoubtedly *always* include contradictory worldviews and truths. Though marriage may bring an end to *some* of the challenges articulated in this study (i.e. finding a spouse, not having an outlet for physical desires), others like how to traverse gendered spaces will remain, leading to the seemingly infiniteness of the third space.

CULTURAL EVOLUTION

Though in different ways, one thing is apparent, the struggles and experiences of this generation are contributing to culture change, both within the hegemonic ideals of American Muslim communities (e.g. no dating) and within the American landscape. Muslim young adults are negotiating, contesting and challenging the assumptions behind both the Muslim ideologies and the cultural systems they encounter. They are choosing their own path. For example, Rahma and Isam's impending intercultural marriage serves as an example for those Muslim communities who practice marital endogamy (which Tariq terms as martial racism). As the first marriage of this kind in their families, they may be able to loosen the traditional hold of marital endogamy on other family members and friends.

Changing the Muslim Community

Young Muslims may bring about cultural change in other ways too. The story of Mirza, who has always desired marriage but did not have money to support a wife and now has money but still no wife, may highlight the need for the Muslim community to come up with ways for young Muslims to get married with temporary assistance from the family or community. Further, women like Tahira, Zahra and Aminah who contemplate marrying non-Muslim men, may force the community to examine the feelings and angst of Muslims who desire marriage but are unable to find a spouse. If they do indeed decide to marry non-Muslims (like other sisters have done), this will naturally change the makeup of the Muslim community in drastic ways. It can lead to several children of mixed-religion households that is if the spouse does not convert to Islam.

While these trends are already occurring, Muslim communities do not appear to address them in an open way. The experiences of these young adults are contributing to major changes in the ways Muslims see themselves now, through the institutions they are constructing (e.g. Seven Shades), and will certainly change the landscape of American Islam within the next 20 years when they inherit the *masjids* and Muslim institutions that their parents have built.

DePaulo (2006) and Stein (1975) would argue that marriage is dying. Yet, this study has shown that for Muslims, marriage is very much alive. It is an important part of Muslim communities and Muslim ways of life and has no markings of slowing down. For Muslims who believe in the afterlife and strive for the afterlife, marriage is still the only way to achieve both a sense of well being (through physical intimacy) and a family.

Yes, many Muslims delay marriage for education, but most do not reject marriage as a whole. Thus a better question would be, is Muslim marriage changing? Does this study on the attitudes of single Muslims highlight any major trends in Muslim marriage? I have already mentioned the stories of those who reject marital endogamy as well as the sisters who consider marrying non-Muslims. However, this data also suggests that given the negative singlehood experiences of current Muslim young adults, the trend for the next generation of Muslim youth may very well be to marry early. To protect their children from struggling to find a spouse, or even from sexualized college experiences, many future parents may decide that it may be in their best interest to allow their children to marry prior to finishing college. In fact, Robert Dannin's work among African-American Muslims reports on the Universal Islamic Brotherhood of Cleveland that conducts teenage marriages to control adolescent sexual behavior (Dannin, 2002).

Marriage for Muslims is alive and well!

Also, the experiences of many Muslim young adults may lead them to experiment with different ways of courtship and loosen the gender segregation of *Masjids* (at least during social events). Perhaps "date night" at the *masjids* will be a way for marriage minded individuals to have fun while getting to know their intended spouse on a deeper level – within a Muslim environment. While I am aware that many Muslims will object to the word "date," and suggest that type of event would be too much like a "club," I am simply suggesting that some how, some way, I anticipate that Muslim leadership will have a different face and community events may change as well.

Changing America

Also, though this study focused on the influences of American culture on American Muslims, the relationship is dialectical. Muslims in college affect their peers and Muslims in the workplace have the ability to influence their co-workers. Sure, the peer culture pushes many to the boundaries of Islam, but several Muslims have found ways to resist these external pressures. Through their resistance, by perhaps limiting relationships with the opposite sex or setting certain boundaries, the attitudes and views of others they encounter may be altered in ways we have yet come to know. It would be interesting to study the non-Muslim friends of Muslims to investigate their views on Islam and what they feel about Muslim lifestyles.

In addition, as much of the discourse in the general American public concerning Muslims revolves around terrorism and war, this exploration may also change the public perception of American Muslims. Non-Muslims will be able to see the everyday real life struggles American Muslims face and also realize most American Muslims are not much different from the average American. They believe in God (like most Americans) and work to create a sense of well being (through physical and emotional desires). The experiences presented here could easily have been those of evangelical Christians (like those of Frietas (2008), Jews, Hindus, Buddhists, Mormons or other religious minorities. Also, we have seen how religion can be a tool of resistance for religious minorities uncomfortable with both racial endogamy and the sexualized nature of popular culture. By enacting a Muslim identity, one may be able to escape these cultural forces.

THE MUSLIM FIRST MYTH

It's great to bounce ideas off of a critical thinker and I thank my older brother Maurice for contributing to this section. We were having a late night chat about being Muslim and we began to discuss the idea of being Muslim first. Throughout this book I have argued that we must examine singlehood with a contextual lens because of racial, ethnic and generational lines of difference. But one thing that we discovered is that the idea of a "Muslim first" mentality just may be a myth. The idea that a person is Muslim before all other characteristics implies that Islam is mutually exclusive to the predominant culture, which is false.

Looking at the history of Islam, we can see that every nation that accepted Islam added it on top of what was already there. If they practiced black magic before Islam, they practiced black magic after Islam. If they were people who liked to hunt game, Islam did not change the way they fed their families. If the women dressed in colorful garments, they did not suddenly adopt black and gray as their preferred style of dress. Yes, those things that were clearly un-Islamic were transformed (like killing baby girls) but typically, Islam was simply an addition to their lives, less something that removed their existing cultures.

The same goes for American Muslims. As we see, some things were common to the brothers and sisters studied just because they were born and raised in an American landscape. Outside of these similarities, it was most often their race/ethnicity that determined the other aspects of their lives. For example, the Desis were more apt to adopt an arranged marriage, and someone like Ali, a Blackamerican was more apt to discuss the effects of slavery on spousal selection. So while these individuals are indeed Muslim, they are *American Muslim + their cultural ethnicity.*

And that is a beautiful thing - that the rain of Islam can reveal a rainbow of interpretations, and peoples. So instead of looking for someway to blend into one solid mass of color, let us begin to acknowledge that the source is One and that it is ok for green to be green and purple to be purple. They are all equal in the sight of the Lord.

LIMITATIONS & NEXT STEPS

Every study has limitations and this one is no different. Exploring Muslim singlehood has been useful to highlight some of these larger issues and reveal some of the cultural changes that occur as a result. I admit that the situation is very complex and as a result, my study may have merely skimmed the surface. To produce a more thorough exploration, a further study could focus on just one or two aspects of singlehood, perhaps courtship and loneliness, or becoming Muslim. Also, this study aimed to give voice to young Muslims and as a result is very rich in empirical data from interviewees. However, in the essence of space, I did not include much data from other community members (parents, Imams and those over 40 year of age). A further study could include more of their views (in their own words rather than the interpretation of their words).

Ethnic backgrounds – while my study was diverse, there were key groups of people who were not represented: Second generation African immigrants, Malaysians, Indonesians and Arab Men. They should be included.

Singlehood a second time around. The experiences of divorcees and those who have lost their spouses would also help to increase our understandings.

Gay and Lesbian Muslims.

One last group that I did not fully investigate were gay and lesbian Muslims. However, just prior to the printing of this first edition, I had the opportunity to talk to one gay Muslim male who provided special insights into the struggles of American gay Muslims. I present his abridged story here with the understanding that any follow up study must explore this topic deeper.

"I'm not really struggling with religion and being gay. I'm gay and I'm Muslim - that's who I am," says Shakir, a 30-year-old African-American lawyer. Raised in a "fairly conservative" Muslim home, Shakir attended an Islamic private school for most of his schooling. He has analytically studied the Quran and Islam for several years and though he questions some of the things he reads, Shakir feels that religiously, his connection to Islam has a lot to do with personality. He says, *"I don't think I'm the type of person that would change religions. If I was born Catholic, I would probably be a gay Catholic."*

Shakir remembers being attracted to boys as young as the age of 6. As he grew older, socialization and gender roles made him long for marriage, a wife and kids because, *"My gayness doesn't work with what everyone expects you to be. To be accepted you need to get married and have kids."* He struggled with his feelings, he states, *"I remember being in Mecca as a 14 year old crying and praying at the kabba to make me straight. Why did I have to be gay?"*

About 10 years after that prayer, Shakir came out to his parents. God sent his answer and the answer was "*Shakir, just be you!*" His parents were shocked and unsupportive. Shakir was initially very hurt and angry by their lack of support and hostile reaction, but he and his parents have since adopted a "don't ask, don't tell" policy when it comes to Shakir's private life. Though it was difficult, Shakir felt it was important to be honest with his parents and he expects his parents to be honest with others too. He told his mom, "*Don't tell your friends that I haven't' found the right woman yet. I'm never going to marry a woman.*"

Living in a society that "*hates gay people*" isn't easy, but Shakir believes most of the opposition to homosexuality comes from socialization; that people have been taught to believe that two people of the same sex loving each other is wrong. Cleary most Muslims state that homosexuality is prohibited in the Quran as well. To that, Shakir asks his fellow Muslims to reinterpret the passages - that the context of the story could very well be lost. He suggests, "*Sodom and Gomorrah wasn't about homosexuality, it was about a depraved city. Literally it was everyone, doing everything. People sleeping with their sisters, swingers, etc. And that's what the story was about more than any specific act.... When those young men showed up at the door, the older men seemed like they were going to rape them. It really sounds like they had malicious intent, not just that they were going to sleep with them.*"

Shakir does not believe being gay is a sin – it is simply the way Allah made him. He takes comfort in the fact that in Islam, there is no intercessor. He lives his life in accordance with what he believes is right and reminds those that judge him that Allah alone will be the judge of us all. For now, Shakir is single but is definitely looking for a long-term committed relationship. He jokes, "*if you have somebody let me know!*" He would love to adopt children and raise a family. A major thing he would like for others to realize is that "*being gay is not a choice.*" Obviously Shakir's story does not represent all gay Muslims, but it highlights just how little we know about American Muslims.

So to close again with my main point: Muslim singlehood is a kind of silent battleground found within the hearts, souls and minds of Muslim young adults. A complex, ambiguous and hybrid place which involves a daily spiritual and emotional *jihad* (struggle), yet is off the radar of much of the greater world. To support single Muslim young adults, we must first assess the situation on the ground. We must discover what the issues are at hand and the only way we can accomplish that task is to ask single Muslims themselves. I hope this study sparks new ideas and conversations around singlehood and other issues of interest to the Muslim community and by extension to the American public as a whole. Naturally, all errors in this book are mine and mine alone.

APPENDICES

A Letter to the Brothers – Halim Naeem

On The Journey to Marriage

So You Wanna Know? ™

APPENDIX I

A LETTER TO THE BROTHERS

By Halim Naeem

This letter is not about preparing to get a woman. It's about how being a man and reclaiming our manhood are what hold a relationship together. There is something very important about manhood and being in positive environments that will foster this manhood. We need to speak more to each other as men and as brothers. We need to speak more to each other about how to properly respect, honor and handle a woman. We need to make sure that those little boys on and off the streets grow up knowing what it is to be a man and to be loved and cared for both by women and especially by a man. We don't know who we are as men and what we are meant to be. Most of us are roaming around confused and disoriented without any desire for a direction of how reach our potential and fulfill our destiny of reclaiming the manhood that was meant to be ours.

Men are all brothers to each other in the human race whether we act as such or not. So my brothers, I am speaking to all of you. But mostly, this is for my brothers out there who struggle to stay out the bed with someone they desire, who are trying to make ends meet for their families, who try to be the best man they can for their woman but they do not get the support they need. This is for the brothers who have thought about leaving their relationship and starting all over again, this is for my brothers on the street who the system legitimately screwed over. This is for my brothers who are working their butts off so that their children and grandchildren never have to work that hard again.

This is for my brothers who try to explain what manhood means to his woman and she simply does not get it. For my brothers who work as hard as possible but there still not enough money coming in. This is for my brothers out looking for a job, but people do not even call or write a letter to reject them, this is for my brothers in prison who are doing the best they can with the situation God put them in (May God bless you). This is for all the brothers who grew up and their deadbeat fathers did not stay long enough in their life to show them how to be men. This is for my brothers whose women just do not know what a valuable and hot commodity they are.

This is for the brothers who want some time for themselves but life smothers them. For the men who resent the fact that their women are bringing most of the money into the house. For the brothers who are trying to get their life together, for the brothers who had their manhood attacked and torn up by angry women who do not know the first thing about being a man. This is for the brothers who want to make a difference in the world but do not know how to make a difference in themselves. For the brothers who feel like no one in the world knows what they are going through. This is for my brothers who are crippled by the system to a point where they must sell drugs so their families can stay inside a home during below zero degree winters. For the brother who feels like no one in the world has true love and empathy for them.

This is for the brothers who have a crazy woman after him or a crazy woman with him (God help you). Lastly, this is for all my brothers who could not make it with us, who could not be here with us, who had to die or be put away, who had to be laid to rest, who had to be shot, who had to be tortured, who had to be violated, who had to see their families be raped, molested and taken away from them, this is for all my brothers on the street who had a prison cell or a casket waiting for them soon after they came out their mother's womb, I love you all, just like you were my own brothers. This is for all the other brothers whose issues I have not spoken towards as of yet, I apologize.

This letter has come in the right time of my life. I am trying to figure some things out myself, but have learned some of the core things that are needed for a successful relationship. I pray that I learn to implement everything that I am sharing here and that this letter is of some benefit.

Knowing what it takes to be a man and secure in that manhood is so important in building a culture of marriage in all of our communities. More importantly, it makes for healthier marriages that stand the test of time. It is a shame that there are so many women out there looking for real men to be husbands and fathers. Nonetheless, they do not know what that looks like. Therefore, we see many bad decisions being made that actually become a huge burdens on society. For example, teenage pregnancy, fatherless children, child support, etc. these issues not only bring the morale of society to an astronomical low, but it costs society billions of dollars. To prevent these issues we must have healthy families, which begin with healthy marriages, which in turn begin with men knowing how to be men (achieving their *manhood).*

Brothers, the number one thing that keeps a man and a woman together in a relationship or in marriage is *Manhood,* and how that manhood is handled by both parties (the men and women in the relationships). Most women do not know this. It is not femininity that maintains a relationship, though femininity is extremely important, but it is Manhood – I mean whatever you believe deep down in your soul contributes to masculinity. For example, this could be money, attractiveness to women, power, popularity, security, strength, penile size, physical size, sexual ability, status, intelligence, how homophobic you are supposed to be, surpassing your father's accomplishments, being the man that can best satisfy your woman sexually without questioning yourself, being a father, supporting your mother, supporting the people close to you, having something significant that belongs to you, principles you hold, how religious you are, etc. It can be a combination of the items mentioned above or other things that were not mentioned. Regardless of the combination, we as men need to identify what those values are. It is not as simple as one thinks. Sometimes the only way to find out what you define as *manhood* is by living with someone who brings out situations, actions or feelings that you feel are opposite to your definition of Manhood.

Why is Manhood more vital for a relationship than femininity? Because men have a very special and different relationship with gender and gender roles that can and actually do make or break relationships. Thus if not catered to within an acceptable margin, men will simply leave, perform an act to sever the relationship, or make the relationship as miserable as they feel inside about themselves. For women, the three main components that contribute to femininity are beauty (how desirable they look to themselves), attractiveness (how much arousal and desire comes from other men towards her) and intimacy (how much attraction, attention and sought-after emotion comes from her object of desire towards her, and the level of closeness they achieve in their desire towards each other). A few things have to be in place for intimacy to occur such as trust, safety, comfort and internal security. Many times women do not get all their individual femininity needs fulfilled, yet since they are in a relationship with someone they desire and the man is giving the attention and desire to her at a somewhat acceptable level, the relationship is at least tolerable (not optimum, but they can live with it). Brothers, we are not the same way. If we do not get our needs met as men, then somehow, some way we exit the relationship.

This manhood cannot be taught to us by anyone other than another male. Nothing can replace this. A woman may be familiar with the male anatomy and may even know more about it than a man. She may have extensive experience about what it is to be with a man. However a woman will never know what it is to actually be a man inside of the male anatomy. It is this combination that is needed to nurture the true nature of the male and bring about positive and healthy developmental masculinity traits. The reason that many of our brothers are suffering is because of the lack of a male mentor or some type of model that will show us exactly how a healthy man should live life. Without this, there will be no successful relationships. Thus, we have a rate of approximately four out of five women who are single mothers in the Black community. The root of the problem is that both *women and men* do not know what a healthy male figure looks like. It is of utmost importance that we develop programs and create situations that keep our males in the communities and as positive contributors to the society.

Manhood is not something that is simply inherent inside of someone. Since masculinity is largely socialized, then this is something that is developed. This is developed through seeing people who have good relationships, doing positive things in society, treating women with utmost respect and honor and are secure in the fact that they are not only male, but they are also masculine. You can think of it more as an art that is a growing process rather than something you have or do not have. This also implies that it can be done in an infinite amount of ways, people, cultures, and combinations. It is an art. So there is flexibility, yet there are intercultural commonalities that span over healthy masculine development.

The following is a four stage cycle of internal masculine development. These are broad concepts and proposed to be universal to men of mankind. The cycle is specific to different areas of life. Therefore, on some things, we have not achieved as high a level of *manhood* then in other areas of life.

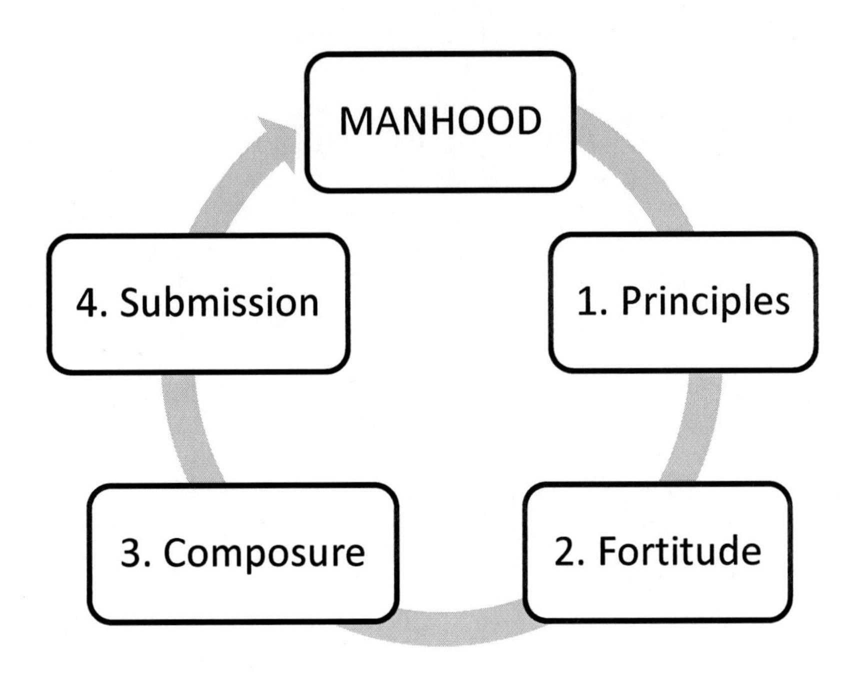

The first stage of achieving complete masculinity is that a male early in life must be taught positive social *principles*. The majority of the male's behavior must comprise of positive social principles (i.e. religious principles, cultural principles, etc). Principles are the base of manhood and the base of men in a relationship. There is a saying in this society that "*A man is only as good as his word.*" Without a principle of integrity for example, there is nothing that can hold a man to a level of honor in dealing with a woman and thus having a healthy relationship. The principles must be there, but they must be valued as a desirable goal to achieve. This value of principles is easy to inject into boys at a very young age. The issue is that many men do not have basic principles that they value and try to enact. The key concept is that we men must see it as a desirable goal to achieve.

Principles must be fostered and modeled thoroughly and consistently for them to become second nature.

The second stage is *fortitude* which is the internal strength to uphold these principles to nearly any obstacle that life brings. This is the base of personality, and one of the main ways we are different from women. We men value strength and power, so much so, that we base our self worth in that. There is another saying: *"If you do not stand for something, then you will fall for anything."* Fortitude is the strength but the internal endurance that will keep a man to his principles no matter what is put in front of him. A woman in a relationship with a man will not like or agree with everything that her man stands for, but if it is something positive, she will respect it. Both men and women resent men who do not have this fortitude to stand for something. The fortitude is there inside all of us, but it needs to be fostered

The third stage is *composure* (self control) which is the ability to not be enslaved to the impulses, the hormones and the emotions which generate foolhardy and irrational behavior. If those things (emotions, hormones, etc.) are used for good and positive behavior, then that is good. This *composure* is a higher level of strength than *fortitude*. When we have the strength to uphold our principles with fortitude, *how* we do so is where composure comes in. We may have the fortitude but we may uphold our principles with violence. That is not a good option if there are other options. *Buddha said "It is a man's own mind, not his enemy or foe, that lures him to evil ways."* It is vital in the relationship that at least one person keep their composure in conflict and other situations. The composure I am speaking of is broader in sense. This is the ability to keep ourselves from acting irrationally, making bad decisions, making rash decisions, overreacting, saying harmful things, etc.

The fourth stage is *submission* which means submitting to God (higher power, broader power, greater power) & one's responsibilities. The greatest of all the responsibilities in this world is the family. In my wife and mine's premarital counseling, the counselor, Imam Ali Suliman said that there was an ancient Arab saying: *"If you submit to your wife, then she will submit to you."* Without submission, there is no perceived need to be responsible or hold ourselves accountable for anything. In our families this means that we submit to the fact that we are married or have kids and contour our lives to the consequences we have given ourselves. It is only then, that a woman will truly submit to you my brothers because in essence, she is submitting to your principles since *you* have done so already. Those who do not agree with your principles and how you uphold and submit to them, will not be relevant to you. What you stand for will repel them. As for those women who are in line with what you are about, they will more easily submit to you -and you to them- which has the components (trust, security, intimacy, etc) of a healthy and long lasting relationship already embedded into it.

Once we are in a complete state of *submission* with *principles, fortitude,* and *composure* in line, then we have achieved *manhood* in its purest sense. We have become people that our wives (or future wives) can lean on. We have become people that our children can lean on. Therefore, when we become complete in our masculine development, we have what it takes to truly say *"till death do us part"* because the characteristics are there for a long and healthy marriage. That's when we become men. If the cycle is cut off or halted then *manhood* is not achieved. My brothers, there is no woman that can imprint this into our being. We need each other so that our families can be built upon us once again. Without us believing that we are men deep down inside, we know that we feel like we are nothing, and others will look upon us the same way. This cannot and will not happen since hopefully, we will have the support of one another.

Sincerely,

Halim Naeem

APPENDIX II

On the Journey to Marriage
A Practical Guide for Ending Muslim Singlehood

While it's great to get married, it's more important to have a *healthy* marriage - one that is mutually fulfilling and lasting. To achieve that, the first step is to become a healthy person within. Letting go of negative thoughts and emotions, forgiving yourself for your shortcomings (and past wrongs), and allowing Allah to guide you is key to this process. I've heard, *"I've been married before, I don't need to prepare for marriage"* as well as "*I don't need to work on myself. I'm straight. I just need a spouse!*" Whether you've been married before, or are looking to get married for the first time, inner reflection is integral to the positive evolution we all desire in our lives.

Use the following exercises to help center your thoughts and behaviors on what it is you truly want in a relationship. You may write in this book or if you prefer, record them in a journal.

1. Purify Your Niyah (pronounced Nee-ya, Intentions)

In a quiet place, ask yourself, "Why am I getting married?" Think of ALL the reasons (physical, emotional, social). If you are getting married for physical reasons only, please reconsider. The divorce rate is too high for us to marry without proper preparation!

2. *What Do I Want For Myself?*

Examine your beliefs, tastes, and values.
What are the top five priorities in your life?
What five things you would like to improve upon?
Where do you see yourself in 5 years?

3. *Act Married!*

If you got married tomorrow, would anything about your everyday daily life routine change? Example: Would you dress differently? Get a different job? Go back to school? Stop hanging around certain people? Think about how getting married may affect your life and consider making those changes now.

4. *What Do You Really Want in a Spouse?*

When I ask this question, people often respond, "I just want someone on their *deen* (religion)." While we know religion should be the top priority, we realize there are several deal breakers for couples. For example, two religiously compatible individuals may be very socially incompatible. Be open and be honest about what you truly desire in a spouse - no matter how seemingly shallow.

Start with the 18 questions at the end of this section to explore your true feelings. Religion: How do you want your family to practice Islam? Socially: What's your idea of a good time? Physically: What's attractive to you?

5. *Get Help Finding That Person!*

Let people know you are ready to get married. Get family and friends involved. Secret, backdoor marriages do not work!
Who do you trust to help you find a spouse and why? If you are already involved with someone, why not set up pre-marital counseling to see if you are compatible?

For Sisters: Find a *wali* (Male Guardian). I recently heard about a marriage between two Muslims in their late 40s. The bride's *wali* was her distant cousin's 15-year-old son. Ladies, that is not a proper *wali*! Get someone who truly has your best interest at heart AND can talk to the brother on your behalf. The brother should know that you are not alone in this process!

For Brothers: If you are worried about how to approach a sister, please ask an Imam or other member of the community. Most single sisters are open to someone inquiring about them. Also, don't be afraid to check out her background as well, not every beautiful sister will make a beautiful wife.

6. *You See Someone You Are Interested in..... Now What?*

- Make Dua (A Prayer)!
- Ask a friend/imam/ other community member to inquire about the person's marital status, personality and likes/dislikes.
- Make Dua again to Allah to purify your heart and to assist you in your journey.
- If the feeling is mutual, arrange a meeting with you, the person, a representative from their side and a representative from your side. (Usually family or a wali). Discuss the important things (deal breakers) BEFORE emotions are involved! It can be easy to develop romantic feelings for someone who may not be the best spouse for you. This also ensures that it is clear that the purpose of the meeting is to decide if you would like further contact for marriage. Getting other people involved from the beginning is a safeguard for both of you. Don't be afraid to ask the tough questions.

7. *Getting to know each other.*

Take your time! Use the questions below as a guide for discussion.
Try to observe each other in natural settings.
Meet each other's families.
Pray! Continue to pray for guidance throughout the process.
Be open about your feelings.
If you decide the person is not right for you, break it off. Don't keep it going.
Try to meet in public and be God Conscious! Be aware that you are getting married both for your pleasure and for Allah's pleasure. Don't do

anything that will jeopardize your standing with Allah. The desire for sex is strong, but waiting a few more months won't kill you! You're getting married for life, not to fulfill the desire in a few moments.

7. *Engagement & Premarital Counseling*

You have determined that this is someone you would like to marry. InshaAllah your families have met (even if your family is non-Muslim or unsupportive, it is important to get family involvement in the process of getting married).

Pray for Guidance and listen to the answer (look up the *Istikhara* prayer for guidance). At this stage you and your fiancé must go to pre-marital counseling with either a qualified Imam or marriage counselor. Don't skip this step. The more you prepare for marriage, the stronger it will be. There are several types of pre-marital counseling but we suggest having a minimum of 3-5 sessions prior to the marriage. Reach out to non-Muslim marriage counselors as well, they have a lot of useful advice and are highly trained in this area.

8. *The Marriage*

Prepare the Marriage contract. (See Surah 4, An-Nisa)
Decide what is important to you. The contract can be as detailed or simple as you like it. For example: Husband is responsible for the cleaning of the home and the wife will be responsible for the cooking. Or, we will not move out of state without a mutual agreement. Or we will not have overnight guests without mutual agreement. The contract can include anything you two mutually agree upon.
Mahr: The couple should come to an agreement for a dowry. What do you consider a suitable dowry? Include this in the contract.

Congratulations! Enjoy your marriage and continue to do exercises to strengthen your relationship. Believe me, marriage is beautiful, but it is also hard work. Don't expect it to be a breeze like you see (or don't see) in the movies.

A list of resources will be available online at www.niyah.net.

APPENDIX III

So You Wanna Know ™ Book Version - 18 Questions

Getting to Know Your Future Spouse (or family member) is Just a Card Away!

Contributions by Cheryl El-Amin, LMSW

Object:
The following question cards cover a wide range of categories: Marriage, Conflict Resolution, Money, Family, Friends, Expressions, Health, etc. The entire game can be purchased on our website at www.niyah.net. For now, you can copy these pages or cut them from the book and place the question cards in a container. There are over 175 question cards, including blanks in the companion set to this book. A set of 18 cards on various subjects are provided below (the full game would be played with 21 at a time). Remember, the card(s) you select are destined for you…Alhamdulillah!

How to Play: Take turns pulling the cards; read the card aloud, reflect for a minute and state your answer. If you pull an "**ask me anything**" card, the person on your right can make up his or her own question. If you pull a **blank card** you get to speak on a topic of your choice. If you don't feel comfortable answering this or any question, just say " I pass" and move on to the next person or a new question if you wish (no compulsion).

Try not to get bogged down in long answers. Use an egg or other timer to limit responses to no more than 3 minutes, then move on to the next person. After 6 questions have been answered, allow 2-3 minutes for comments from others. Or you can just wait until all 18 have been answered.

Limit the exercise to no more than 18 questions at one sitting. Trust that Allah will guide your selections; leading you to learn what is important for that particular time. In order to cover the full range of topics, play the question game several times (perhaps keeping previously answered questions out). People and relationships change over time. Return to the question game periodically before and during the marriage to become acquainted or re-acquainted with each other in a fun way! SAMPLE:

MARRIAGE DESCRIBE A "GOOD" MARRIAGE. CITE REAL LIFE EXAMPLES.	? HOW WILL I KNOW WHEN I KNOW YOU? HOW WILL YOU KNOW WHEN YOU KNOW ME?
FAMILY DEFINE THE HUSBAND'S ROLE.	MARRIAGE WHAT ARE YOUR EXPECTATIONS OF MARRIAGE?
AFTER MARRIAGE HOW WILL YOU EXPRESS ROMANTIC FEELINGS? WHY?	GOALS WHAT ARE YOUR SHORT TERM GOALS? WHAT PERIOD OF TIME? (I.E. DAY(S); MONTH(S); YEAR(S)?)
CONFLICT RESOLUTION WHEN DO YOU THINK IT IS APPROPRIATE TO INITIATE MEDIATION IN MARRIAGE?	FAMILY DO YOU WANT TO PRACTICE POLYGAMY? WHY OR WHY NOT?

? WHY HAVE YOU CHOSEN ME AS YOUR FUTURE SPOUSE?	**LIFESTYLE** WHAT ARE YOUR HOBBIES?
? DON'T ASK ME ANYTHING ABOUT_______!!	? I'M HAPPIEST WHEN I?
RELIGION WHAT IS THE ROLE OF RELIGION IN YOUR LIFE?	**RELIGION** THE DIFFERENCE BETWEEN RELIGION AND SPIRITUALITY IS_____ I CONSIDER MYSELF MORE___________.
LIFESTYLE WHAT DO YOU LIKE TO DO FOR FUN?	**INTERPRETATION** WHAT DOES "BEAT THEM LIGHTLY" MEAN TO YOU?
RELIGION WHAT TYPE OF MUSLIM/ISLAMIC VOLUNTEER ACTIVITIES DO YOU PARTICIPATE IN? WHY?	? ASK ME ANYTHING.

GLOSSARY

Ahadith: The plural of Hadith (see Hadith)

Adhan (Arabic): The call to prayer.

Al-Akhirah: After-Life, Hereafter, Next World. The term embraces the following ideas: That man is answerable to God; That the present order of existence will someday come to an end; That when that happens, God will bring another order into being in which He will resurrect all human beings, gather them together and examine their conduct, and reward them with justice and mercy; That those who are reckoned good will be sent to Paradise whereas the evil-doers will be consigned to Hell; That the real measure of success or failure of a person is not the extent of his prosperity in the present life, but his success in the Next.

Alhamdulillah: English transliteration for the Arabic; meaning: All praise be to God.

Allah: English transliteration for the Arabic; meaning: The One God.

Blackamerican: Term coined by Dr. Sherman Jackson in *Islam and the Blackamerican.* It refers to the group of people commonly known as African-Americans.

Desi: Colloquial term used to refer to peoples of South Asian descent (namely Pakistanis and Indians)

Deen (Arabic): Religion

Dua': English transliteration for the Arabic; meaning: Non-obligatory free form prayer or supplication that can be done by anyone at any time without rules and regulation pertaining.

Dunya: Worldly Life. The current life on earth.

Eid: English transliteration for the Arabic; meaning: holiday or celebration. The main festivals of the Muslim year are Eid al-Fitr (commemorates the completion of *Ramadan)* and Eid al-Adha (commemorates the Hajj and Prophet Abraham's devotion and willingness to sacrifice his son for God).

Hadith: English transliteration for the Arabic; meaning: The written collection of the teachings and sayings of the Prophet Muhammad (s.a.w.), which are verified by authentic sources and compiled in reputable books of the collections of *Hadith*, such as in the books of Sahih Muslim or Sahih Bukhari, etc.

Hajj: Fifth pillar of Islam. The Muslim pilgrimage to Makkah.

Halal: Permissible.

Haram: Forbidden.

Hijab (He-jab): The literal meaning is a curtain or barrier. Colloquially it is used to refer to the headscarf many Muslim women wear.

Hijabi: the colloquial term to define a woman who wears *hijab* (headscarf)

Imam: Typically a leader of Salat (formal prayer). Popularly, can also refer to scholar or leaders of a community.

Insha'Allah: "If Allah Wills"

ISNA: Islamic Society of North America (founded in 1982), is probably the largest Muslim organization in North America.

Jazaku Allahu Khair: (or Jazakallah khyrun) English transliteration for the Arabic; meaning: May God reward you for [the] good.

Jum'ah (Arabic): Literally "Friday". Jumah refers to the Muslim Friday prayers

LOL: Internet Chat abbreviation for "Laughing Out Loud"

LMAO: Internet Chat abbreviation for "Laughing My Ass Off". Even people like me who do not curse sometimes write this abbreviation.

Mahr: Bridal gift that which the husband is required to make to his bride. It is settled between the two spouses at the time of marriage and symbolizes the financial responsibility that a husband assumes towards his wife by virtue of entering into the contract of marriage.

Mahram: A man whom a woman can never marry because of closeness of relationship (e.g. father, brother, uncle, son, etc.). Her husband is also her Mahram.

Mashallah: English transliteration for the Arabic; meaning: God has willed it.

Masjid: Mosque

MSA: Muslim Student's Association

Musalla: Prayer room or space (usually carpeted) designated for prayer.

Muslim: English transliteration of the Arabic; meaning: believer (i.e. believer in God). Also, the name of a book of the collections of Hadith, "Sahih Muslim."

Muslima: Muslim Woman

Nikah: The *Nikah* is the Islamic marriage contract which binds the couple as a union in the sight of God.

Niqab: Face veil that some Muslim women wear covering the face except the eyes

Niqabi: The colloquial term used to refer to women who wear the *niqab*

Niyah: Intentions

OMG: Internet abbreviation for "Oh My God"

PBUH: Peace be upon him. Used interchangeably with (saw) to invoke blessings after the name of the Prophet Muhammad (pbuh) is mentioned.

Quran: Also spelled Koran. The compilation of the revelations Muslims believe were revealed to the Prophet Muhammad (Peace be upon him)

***Ramadan*:** *Ramadan* is the Islamic month of fasting.

Salat: Second pillar of Islam. Formal ritualistic prayer

(SAW): English abbreviation of the transliteration of the Arabic phrase, "Sallallahu alayhi wa salaam"; meaning: The peace and blessing of God be upon him. This is said whenever the name of prophet Muhammad (S.A.W.) is mentioned or read. In English it is written (pbuh).

Sawm: Fasting

Shahadah: First pillar of Islam. Ashaddu an la illaha ilallah wa ashaddu anna Muhammadar Rasulullah - English transliteration for the Arabic; meaning: I bear witness that there is no god except God, and I bear witness that Muhammad is the [last] Messenger of God.

Sheikh: Literally "an old man", but religiously a male scholar

Shi'a: Shi'a Muslims comprise the second- largest denomination of Muslims.

Sunnah: English transliteration for the Arabic; meaning: The traditions and practices of the Prophet Muhammad (s.a.w.) that are not only recorded in the books of Sahih Muslim and Sahih Bukhari but have been in practice since the day of the Prophet (s.a.w.) until the present.

Sunni: The largest overall denomination of Muslims, Sunnis are the majority in most Muslim countries.

Surah: English transliteration for the Arabic; meaning: chapter; as in, "chapter" and verse.

(SWT): English abbreviation of the transliteration of the Arabic phrase, "Subhannah wa t'ala"; meaning: Glory be to the Mighty God.

Ummah: English transliteration for the Arabic; meaning: All of the Muslims collectively; Muslim community.

Wali: Guardian. In reference to marriage, it is often used to refer to male who serves as the protector of the Muslim sister during marriage negotiations.

Walima: Marriage Banquet

Zakat: The third pillar of Islam; Literally "Purification." It is the obligatory charity for all Muslims which amounts to a minimum of 2.5% of an individual's wealth.

Zawaj: Literally means marriage.

Bibliography

Abdo, G. (2006). *Mecca and main street: Muslim life in America after 9/11*. New York: Oxford University Press.

Adamson, L., & Lyxell, B. (1996). Self-concept and questions of life: Identity development during late adolescence. *Journal of Adolescence, 19*(6), 569-582.

Ahmed, L. (1992). *Women and gender in Islam: Historical roots of a modern debate.* Connecticut: Yale University Press.

Ali, A. Y. (1987). *The holy quran: Text translation and commentary.* Tahrike Tarsile Qur'an.

Ali, S. (2005). Why here, why now? Young Muslim women wearing hijāb. *Muslim World, 95*, 515.

Al-Johar, D. (2005). Muslim marriages in America: Reflecting new identities. *The Muslim World, 95*, 557-574.

Amit-Talai, V., & Wulff, H. (1995). *Youth cultures: A cross-cultural perspective.* London: Routledge.

Anderson, B. (1991). *Imagined communities: Reflections on the origin and spread of nationalism.* London and New York: Verso.

Aswad, B. C., & Bilgé, B. (1996). *Family and gender among American Muslims: Issues facing middle eastern immigrants and their descendants.* Philadelphia: Temple University Press.

Aubrey, J. S., Harrison, K., Kramer, L., & Yellin, J. (2003). Variety versus timing: Gender differences in college students' sexual expectations as predicted by exposure to sexually oriented television. *Communication Research, 30*(4), 432.

Badahdah, A. M., & Tiemann, K. A. (2005). Mate selection criteria among Muslims living in America. *Evolution and Human Behavior, 26*(5), 432-440.

Barth, F. (1969). *Ethnic groups and their boundaries.* Boston: Waveland Press.

Ba-Yunus, I., & Kone, K. (2006). *Muslims in the United States.* Westport, Connecticut: Greenwood Press.

Beckwith, H. D., & Morrow, J. A. (2005). Sexual attitudes of college students: The impact of religiosity and spirituality. *College Student Journal, 39*(2), 357-367.

Bhabha, H. (1994). *The location of culture*. London and New York: Routledge.
Brah, A. (1996). *Cartographies of diaspora: Contesting identities*. London and New York: Routledge.
Brah, A. (2007). Travels in negotiations: Difference, identity, politics. *Journal of Creative Communications, 2*(1-2), 245.
Breger, R., & Hill, R. (1998). Introducing mixed marriages. In R. Breger, & R. Hill (Eds.), *Cross-cultural marriage* (pp. 1-32) Oxford International Publishers.
Bucholtz, M. (2002). Youth and cultural practice. *Annual Review of Anthropology, 31*, 525-552.
Carlson, C. I., & Chang, H. H. Identity, acculturation, and adjustment of high school Muslim students in Islamic schools in the USA.
Carolan, M. T., Bagherinia, G., Juhari, R., Himelright, J., & Mouton-Sanders, M. (2000). Contemporary Muslim families: Research and practice. *Contemporary Family Therapy, 22*(1), 67-79.
Chait Barnett, R., Gareis, K. C., Boone James, J., & Steele, J. (2003). Planning ahead: College seniors' concerns about career–marriage conflict. *Journal of Vocational Behavior, 62*(2), 305-319.
Chaitin, J. (2004). My story, my life, my identity. *International Journal of Qualitative Methods, 3*(4), 1.
Childs, E. C. (2005). *Navigating interracial borders: Black-white couples and their social worlds.* Rutgers University Press.
Cohen, S. (2002). *Folk devils and moral panics: The creation of the mods and rockers.* Routledge.
Cole, D., & Ahmadi, S. (2003). Perspectives and experiences of Muslim women who veil on college campuses. *Journal of College Student Development, 44*(1), 47-66.
Collins, R. L., Elliott, M. N., Berry, S. H., Kanouse, D. E., Kunkel, D., Hunter, S. B., et al. (2004). Watching sex on television predicts adolescent initiation of sexual behavior. *Pediatrics, 114*(3)
Cox, F. D. (1967). *Youth, marriage and the seductive society* (Second ed.). Dubuque, Iowa: Wm. C. Brown Company Publishers.
D'Alisera, J. A. (2004). *An imagined geography: Sierra Leonean Muslims in America.* University of Pennsylvania Press.
Dannin, R. (2002). *Black pilgrimage to Islam* Oxford University Press US.
Darrington, J., Piercy, K. W., & Niehuis, S. (2005). The social and cultural construction of singlehood among young, single Mormons. *The Qualitative Report, 10*(4), 639-661.

Davies, L. (2003). Singlehood: Transitions within a gendered world. *Canadian Journal on Aging, 22*(4), 343-352.

DePaulo, B. M. (2006). *Singled out: How singles are stereotyped, stigmatized, and ignored, and still live happily ever after.* St. Martin's Press.

Douglas, M. (2002). *Purity and danger: An analysis of concept of pollution and taboo.* New York: Routledge.

Dwyer, C. (2000). Negotiating diasporic identities: Young British south Asian Muslim women. *Women's Studies International Forum, 23*(4), 475-486.

Ehrmann, W. (1959). *Premarital dating behavior.* Holt.

Erikson, E. H. (1968). *Identity: Youth and crisis* WW Norton & Company.

Ewing, K. P. (1998). Crossing borders and transgressing boundaries: Metaphors for negotiating multiple identities. *Ethos, 26*(2), 262-267.

Farmer, A. (1998). *The rich single life: Abundance, opportunity, and purpose in god.* Gathersburg, MD: Sovereign Grace Ministries.

Feldon, B. (2002). *Living alone and loving it: A guide to relishing the solo life.* Simon & Schuster.

Fisherkeller, J. E. (1997). Everyday learning about identities among young adolescents in television culture. *Anthropology & Education Quarterly, 28*(4), 467-492.

Forman, S. (1994). *Diagnosing America: Anthropology and public engagement.* Michigan: University of Michigan Press.

Freitas, D. (2008). *Sex and the soul: America's college students speak out about hookups, romance, and religion on campus.* New York: Oxford University Press.

Garofoli, J. (2007, Monday, June 18). Teen magazine addresses challenges of being Muslim girl in United States. *San Francisco Chronicle*

Geertz, C. (1973). *The interpretation of cultures: Selected essays.* Basic Books.

Geertz, C., & Banton, M. (1966). *Religion as a cultural system.* Tavistock.

Gilliat-Ray, S. (1998). Multiculturalism and identity: Their relationship for British Muslims. *Journal of Muslim Minority Affairs, 18*(2), 347-354.

Glenn, N., & Marquardt, E. (2001). *Hooking up, hanging out, and hoping for Mr. Right.* New York: Institute for American Values.

Graff, E. J. (2003). What is marriage for? *New England Law Review, 38*, 541.

Grewal, Z. A. (2008). Marriage in colour: Race, religion and spouse selection in four American mosques. *Ethnic and Racial Studies, 99999*(1), 1-23.

Haddad, Y. Y. (2002). *Muslims in the west: From sojourners to citizens.* Oxford University Press US.

Haddad, Y. Y., & Esposito, J. L. (1998). *Islam, gender, and social change.* Oxford University Press US.

Haddad, Y. Y., & Lummis, A. T. (1987). *Islamic values in the United States: A comparative study.* Oxford University Press.

Haddad, Y. Y., Moore, K. M., & Smith, J. I. (2006). *Muslim women in America: The challenge of Islamic identity today.* Oxford University Press.

Haeri, S. (1989). *Law of desire: Temporary marriage in Shi'a Islam.* Syracuse, NY: Syracuse University Press.

Hall, K. (2002). *Lives in translation: Sikh youth as British citizens.* University of Pennsylvania Press.

Hall, S. (1990). Cultural identity and diaspora. *Identity: Community, Culture, Difference, 2*, 222-237.

Hall, S., & Du Gay, P. (1996). *Questions of cultural identity.* London: Sage.

Halperin, R. H., & Scheld, S. (2007). Introduction: Youth engage the city and global culture. *City & Society, 19*(2), 169-178.

Holland, D. C., & Eisenhart, M. A. (1990). *Educated in romance: Women, achievement, and college culture.* Chicago: University Of Chicago Press.

Huntington, S. P. (2004). *Who are we? The challenges to America's national identity.* Simon & Schuster.

Jackson, S. A. (2005). *Islam and the blackamerican: Looking toward the third resurrection.* New York: Oxford University Press.

Karim, J. (2005). Between immigrant Islam and black liberation: Young Muslims inherit global Muslim and African American legacies. *Muslim World, 95*(4), 497-513.

Khan, S. (2000). *Muslim women: Crafting a north American identity. Florida:* University Press of Florida.

Kondo, D. K. (1990). *Crafting selves: Power, gender, and discourses of identity in a Japanese workplace.* Chicago: University Of Chicago Press.

Kusserow. (1999). De-homogenizing American individualism: Socializing hard and soft individualism in Manhattan and queens. *Ethos, 27*(2), 210.

Leonard, K. I. (2003). *Muslims in the United States: The state of research.* New York: Russell Sage Foundation.

Longmore, M. A., Manning, W. D., & Giordano, P. C. (2001). Preadolescent parenting strategies and teens' dating and sexual initiation: A longitudinal analysis. *Journal of Marriage and Family, 63*(2), 322-335.

Madison, D. S. (2005). *Critical ethnography: Method, ethics, and performance.* Sage Publications Inc.

Maira, S. (2002). *Desis in the house: Indian American youth culture in New York city.* Philadelphia: Temple University Press.

Marshall, P. (2007). American Islam by Paul M. Barrett. *Commentary, New York American Jewish Committee, 123*(2), 78.

McCloud, A. B. (1995). *African American Islam.* New York: Routledge.

McMurthie, B. (2001). For many Muslim students, college is a balancing act. *Chronicle of Higher Education*

Mir, S. (2006). *Constructing Third Spaces: American Muslim Undergraduate Women's Hybrid Identity Construction*

Moffatt, M. (1989). *Coming of age in New Jersey: College and American culture.* Rutgers University Press.

Moore, K. (2007). Muslims in the United States: Pluralism under exceptional circumstances. *Annals of the American Academy of Political and Social Science, 612*(1), 116.

Naber, N. (2005). Muslim first, Arab second: A strategic politics of race and gender. *Muslim World, 95*(4), 479-495.

Naguib, S. A. (2003). Young, European and Muslim. *Rapport Fra IKS-Seminar i Berlin 10 – 14. November 2001*

Nanda, S., & Warms, R. L. (2002). *Cultural anthropology* Wadsworth/Thomson Learning.

Patel, E. (2003). On nurturing a modern Muslim identity: The institutions of the Aga Khan development network. *Cross Currents, 53*(2), 209.

Peek, L. (2005). Becoming Muslim: The development of a religious identity. *Sociology of Religion, 66*(3), 215.

Raffaelli, M. (2005). Adolescent dating experiences described by Latino college students. *Journal of Adolescence, 28*(4), 559-572.

Rattansi, A., & Phoenix, A. Rethinking youth identities: Modernist and postmodernist frameworks. *Identity, 5*(2), 97-123.

Ravuvu, A. (1978). Research responsibilities in the pacific. A local viewpoint. In A. Mamak, & G. McCall (Eds.), *Paradise postponed: Essays on research and development in the south pacific.* (pp. 73-77). Australia: Perfamon Press.

Rouse, C., & Hoskins, J. (2004). Purity, soul food, and sunni Islam: Explorations at the intersection of consumption and resistance. *Cultural Anthropology, 19*(2), 226-249.

Rouse, C. M. (2004). *Engaged surrender: African American women and Islam.* University of California Press.

Saed, K. (2005). On the edge of becoming. *Living Islam out loud: American Muslim women speak* () Beacon Press.

Schmidt, G. (2004). Islamic identity formation among young Muslims: The case of Denmark, Sweden and the United States. *Journal of Muslim Affairs, 24*(1).

Schneider, D. M. (1980). *American kinship: A cultural account* University of Chicago Press.

Schwedler, J. (2001). Islamic identity: Myth, menace, or mobilizer? *SAIS REVIEW, 21*(2), 1-18.

Sciolino, E. and Mekhennet, S. (2008, In Europe, debate over Islam and virginity. *New York Times,* pp. June 11.

Sokefeld, M. (1999). Debating self, identity, and culture in anthropology. *Current Anthropology, 40*(4), 417.

Stein, P. J. (1975). Singlehood: An alternative to marriage. *Family Coordinator, 24*(4), 489-502.

Stein, P. J. (1981). *Single life: Unmarried adults in social context* .St. Martin's Press.

Stewart, J. (2005). *The single girl's manifesta: Living in a stupendously superior single state of mind.* Sourcebooks, Inc.

Stoller, P. (1989). *The taste of ethnographic things: The senses in anthropology.* University of Pennsylvania Press.

Stryker, S., & Burke, P. J. (2000). The past, present, and future of an identity theory. *Social Psychology Quarterly, 63*(4), 284-297.

Thornton, A. (1990). The courtship process and adolescent sexuality. *Journal of Family Issues, 11*(3), 239.

Thornton, A., Axinn, W. G., & Hill, D. H. (1992). Reciprocal effects of religiosity, cohabitation, and marriage. *The American Journal of Sociology, 98*(3), 628.

Turner, R. B. (2003). *Islam in the African American experience* Indiana University Press.

Turning Muslim in Texas. www.turntoislam.com . [Video/DVD]

Twenge, J. M. (2006). *Generation me: Why today's young Americans are more confident, assertive, entitled--and more miserable than ever before.* Free Press.

Upton, C. (1988). *Doorkeeper of the heart: Versions of Rabi'a.* New York: Pir Press.

Webber, I. L. (2007). *The single girl's guide.* Summersdale.

Wilce, J. M. (1998). Communicating multiple identities in Muslim communities: An introduction. *Ethos, 26*(2), 115-119.

Yamani, M. (1998). Cross-cultural marriage within Islam: Ideals and reality. In Berger and Hill (eds), *Cross-Cultural Marriage: Identity and Choice.* New York: Oxford.

Yankelovich, D. (1998). How American individualism in evolving. *The Public Perspective, February/March.*

Yip, A. K. T. (2006). Resurgent Islam: A sociological approach. *British Journal of Sociology, 57*(3), 540-542.

Zine, J. (2001). Muslim youth in Canadian schools: Education and the politics of religious identity. *Anthropology & Education Quarterly, 32*(4), 399-423.

GIRLS EDUCATION IN WEST AFRICA

The proceeds from the first 300 copies of this book will go directly to support a fact-finding mission to establish a Girls Education Project in Sierra Leone. The Niyah Company is collaborating with Senegal's www.10000girls.org to accomplish this task.

For more info contact Zarinah or visit
www.niyah.net in 2009
Thank You

THE AUTHOR

Zarinah El-Amin Naeem, M.A. is an anthropologist whose current research focuses on contemporary issues facing Muslims in America. She is also the founder of The Niyah Company specializing in "Momentous Events and Commodities to Enliven Your Soul." Her life mission is to "create a world culture of love."

In addition to speaking and writing, Zarinah is a community organizer, an avid international traveler, enjoys tennis, meeting new people and learning more about Allah's beautiful creation. She is married to Halim Naeem, a doctoral candidate in psychology and the president of Seven Shades (www.sevenshades.org). Together they live in Kalamazoo, Michigan and have one cute and inquisitive son, Sufyan.

Please direct all inquires, questions, and comments to her at
zarinahelamin@gmail.com
www.niyah.net coming 2009